I0154729

Breaking The Silence
Generational Curse Breakers

Karen Pless Gaines

All rights reserved. No part of this book may be produced in any form or by any electronic or mechanical means including information storage and retrieval systems—except in the case of brief quotations embodied in critical articles or reviews—without permission in writing to the publisher, Karen Pless Gaines

The characters and events portrayed in this book are fictional, meaning no real name are used except with permission. Any similarity to real persons, living or dead, is purely coincidental and not intended by the author.

The information used to write this book was public knowledge and is cited in the back of the book. For privacy reasons, real names have not been used in the making of this book.

Published by Karen Pless Gaines Toccoa Georgia,
karenplessgaines@outlook.com

Copyright © 2025 Karen Pless Gaines

All rights reserved.

ISBN: 979-8-9879003-1-4

DEDICATION

This book is dedicated to my girls for the countless hours spent diligently conducting research for the writing of this book. I express my deepest gratitude to my daughter, Kiara Espinoza, my daughter-in-law, Hannah Neubold Espinoza, and my cousin, Brandie Fowler. Your unwavering support has been instrumental in answering the call for this work. I want to acknowledge that without your invaluable contributions, I would not have been able to reach this point. I am truly appreciative of the late nights, adventurous road trips, and the collaborative efforts in searching through cemeteries. The dedication and hard work we put in have undeniably paid off.

CONTENTS

CONTENTS

ACKNOWLEDGMENTS

I would like to express my deepest gratitude to my Lord and Savior, Jesus Christ, without whom none of this would be possible. I am incredibly thankful for my son, Preston, whose unwavering assistance has been invaluable in resolving my technical challenges. I am also grateful to Joseph Tomlin for willingly taking on extra responsibilities, allowing me to have more free time. To my husband, Kevin, thank you for your unwavering support in all that I do in the service of God. Your understanding and support during my absences mean the world to me. Brandie Fowler, Kiara Espinoza, and Hannah Neubold Espinoza, I am immensely thankful for your tireless dedication to helping me with this project. Your contributions have been instrumental in its swift completion. I am also deeply appreciative of everyone who keeps me in their prayers—your prayers sustain me each day. And to those who purchase my books, your support is not just a driving force, but a lifeline to my writing. May God bless each and every one of you for the love and encouragement you have shown me in fulfilling His purpose for my life. **********************************

Prelude

The Grave Robbing Generational Curse Breakers

As they stood in the cemetery looking around, thoughts raced through their minds. What were they doing here? What exactly are they looking for? Did this place deeply hold the answers, the missing links in their quest for redemption? The ladies were unsure but knew one thing— they had to keep going. Their lives depended on it. Their children and their grandchildren depended on these exact moments in time. Moments when fear of the unknown was screaming for them to turn around, but the still small voice urged them on. These four ladies were going to succeed where others had failed; they were going to break these generational curses that had plagued their family for so long. Then, they would help others do the same. Armed with determination, wit, charm, and the power of the Holy Ghost, they pushed forward, turning over every stone in their path and chopping down trees with deep roots. That is where the problem starts—the roots. They knew they had to reach the root of the problem to expose it and destroy it. There was no doubt that they would make a lot of enemies along the way. Souls saved along the way would make it all worth the hurt, heartache, and pain. These ladies were the Grave Robbing Curse Breakers.

It is important to note that they did not disturb any graves while they were in the graveyard. The grave robbing part of their name is due to the nature of their task. When we are sinners or even Christians, we can be oppressed. Oppression is, in fact, a grave we sometimes enter and cannot find a way out of. These four women are tasked with helping others escape this grave. By assisting them to break the curses on their lives and their bloodline. As the saying goes, "Blood runs deep." When our ancestors commit a crime, sin, or injustice, it can also influence our lives, especially when we do not realize that it has been and may still be committed today. Have you ever stopped to wonder why certain families are more prone to abuse (any form)? One that is prominent in today's world is molestation and rape. A family member molested a young child, that child grows up and does the same, and their victim does the same. This cycle (curse) will continue until someone finally stands up and says, "NO MORE!" "THIS CURSE ENDS WITH ME." They do not sin and renounce it; therein, the curse is broken.

But I am getting ahead of myself here. Let me introduce four ladies: Judah (Judez), Noa, Jael, And me—Galilee (Gal). Looking at us, we do not exactly look like much; we do not look like we fit this assignment, but God loves to use the ones that people think are underdogs in the fight. See David and Goliath (1 Samuel 17: 20-50), spoiler—David wins. Judah is short with dark raven hair and dark chocolate eyes; she still has that youthful roundness to her face and short stature. Her heart is both bold and soft, and both are attributes that she needs to fulfill this assignment. She truly wears her heart on her sleeve; if she loves you—there is no mistaking it. Noa is also short in stature with darker hair, light eyes, and a smile that will light up a room. She comes from a rough upbringing, so she is a little rough around the edges and sometimes a little cagey. In the end, she has a heart of gold. Much like Judez, these attributes will work in Noa's favor on this mission. Jael is named after, you guessed it— the woman in the Bible who drove a stake through a man's head (Judges 4:17-22; 5:2-31). And much like her namesake, Jael has had a rough life. She is still joyful and at peace; she has confronted her demons and has broken free. Jael is the ringleader, slightly taller than Noa and Judez, firm in stance, and has lots of wisdom, and she will not hesitate to take a stake to the devil. She is training this group of misfits to do the same. Last, we come to Galilee, you can call me Gal. I am the tallest of the group and also the clumsiest. I am a prayer warrior by call. Children are drawn to me. I lack the youthfulness of Noa and Judez, but I make up for it in wisdom. I grew up in what many would consider a war zone at home. So much like Noa, I can be cagey and distant. But like Judez, I also wear my heart on my sleeve.

You may be asking how we found each other. Well, Judez, Jael, and I are blood family. Jael (Karen) is Judez (Kiara) 's mother. And I (Galilee—Brandie) am their cousin. Noa (Hannah) is also part of the family but in a slightly unusual way. God sent Noa to us; she fell in love with Jael's son, Thaddeus (Preston). They have a son named Jeremiah (Parker). He is three years old but is wise beyond his years. At times, Jeremiah gets this look in his eyes like he is staring into your soul; he is a susceptible child. Thaddeus is called for missionary work, and he is already a firecracker. He is still young and likes to goof and have fun, but he truly has a lion's heart and an elephant's wit. He tends to act aloof but pays attention, observes, and absorbs more information than you'd think. This little family is truly going to do remarkable things. They are robbing graves and storming the gates of hell with armies of angels surrounding them and the hand of God on their lives.   By—Brandie Fowler

Breaking Free

Abuse and pain linger there.
Raped at a young age, innocence lost,
My soul's battle, a heavy cost.
Thoughts of suicide, a haunting ghost.
From 2015 to 2022, I boast.
But now I see with clear eyes,
The roots of our family's lies.
Curses weighing heavy on our fate,
Sin's grip seals our state.
Through research, through study,
We strive to break bonds muddy.
No longer victims, we stand tall.
Breaking the cycle, righting it all
Family curses may still lurk,
But with knowledge and love, we work
In the darkness, we find light
Turning all our pain into might.
With each step, we heal and grow.
In our hearts, love starts to flow.
Abuse and pain may have been our past,
But now we're free—free at last.
With courage and strength, we face the day,
In our own unique and powerful way.
So let us rise above the pain,
And let our love forever reign
For, in the end, we will see,
That we are stronger than we ever believed to be.

By: Hannah Neubold Espinoza

It Stops Here

How to go about this road we're on—
Full of lost wonders that's never been told.
Oh, what curses my kin have hidden,
That has hurst us all deep within.

Murderers, drunkards, and all their lustful ways
Will come back to bite them—once we've had our say.

Us four together—
Together as one…
The cast outs, the broken,
The black sheep has won.

The sinful disguise can't hush us no more.
It's time to reveal what's hid behind the doors.

My generation and generations to come,
Won't have to endure the torture you've done.

God raised us up
As we scream from the rooftops
Your secrets are out
The curses now stop.

By: Kiara Espinoza

Tombstones Speak

*If tombstones could speak,
what stories would they tell?
Would we hear of glorious triumphs?
or the sorrow of how from grace they fell?
*Would we hear of laughter and joy
from a love-filled life?
Or would a life of pain, anger, and disappointment
be what we hear of?
*Would they speak of children's laughter and
the pitter-patter of little feet?
Or would they tell of children's anguish
and how they cried themselves to sleep?
*Just listen-they tell more stories
than you could realize.
Look closely—as the stories unfold
right before your eyes.
*A life without Christ
is plain to see,
in the disheveled graves
hidden in bushes and trees.
*What pain did they bring
to deserve separation?
While family close by
donned flowers of celebration.
*Someday if time holds out,
You, too, will say farewell.
as people stroll through to visit,
What stories will your tombstone tell?

Chapter One

Introduction

The glass shatters. Listen to the cracking grinding as it erupts—listen closely and hear it jingle in shards on the ground. Do you hear it? Can you feel the release of pressure as the breath of life comes rushing to rescue you? No more caught in the airless tank of oppression, depression, and anxiety. Gulp in the air, feel the release— capture it—inhale it deeply; you are free. Free from the curse that was strangling you, in capturing you—holding you a prisoner. A prisoner of guilt, shame, and regret attached to your name—and yet you did no wrong—not directly anyway. You only know what you have been taught. Behaviors and actions passed down from generation to generation to you, but what if I told you that today you can be free—free from the bondage of the past—free from generational curses—free from the sins that keep you entangled in the curses of the past? That is what we will discuss in this book: defining a generational curse and how to break free once and for all.

It took me many years to realize the knowledge I will be putting on the pages of this book. Not that I was completely unaware that something was amiss. However, I couldn't quite put my finger on the problem. Then, I decided to get serious with God. I wanted more than to know about him. I wanted to KNOW him. I wanted a relationship—a deep relationship like I have never had before. So, I asked him to show me who he was. I wanted to know everything. As I opened my heart to receive, he poured in the light of knowledge and wisdom of the heart of him. This light revealed things about myself that I didn't like, things I needed to change. I started to see things differently—I saw him differently—then I saw me differently. Who I was before disgusted me so much that I had to let him remold me. I had been back in church at that time for about ten years. But I felt like such a hypocrite when realizing that I had only been going through the motions and was not really in a relationship with Jesus Christ.

Have you, too, come to this knowledge? Have you noticed that something isn't right, but you don't know what that might be? We will delve deep into what a generational curse is as we go through these pages. You will learn what to look for in your life and your family's life that keeps these curses attached to you. I'm also going to use some of my research into my own family to give examples of how easy it is for us to allow Satan and his demons to keep us blind to what is happening. As you proceed in these pages, remember that you can be free from this bondage. Take action to be the curse breaker in your bloodline. Decide that it ends today. It's easier than you think. God only wants you—all of you, not just part of you.

Before we proceed, I want you to see if any of the things listed below resonate with you or your bloodline. If they do, then you've come to the right place.

- Anger issues (passive-aggressive behavior, irritability, emotional dysregulation, hypertension, inward anger, outward anger, silent anger, etc.)

- Toxic behavior (criticism, defensiveness, self-centeredness, manipulation, unpredictability, lack of responsibility, etc.)
- Family traumas (abuse, divorce, infidelity, grief, arguments, domestic violence, financial issues, distance, etc.)
- Mental illness (depression, anxiety, bipolar, dementia, ADHD, schizophrenia, OCD, etc.)
- History of abuse (either victim of or the abuser)
- Failure after failure—you can't seem to prosper at anything
- Miscarriage or death of infants
- Can't conceive a baby
- Female issues (period problems, cysts, tumors, cancers, etc.)
- Eating disorders (anorexia, bulimia, binge eating disorder, body dysmorphic disorder, food addiction, pica disorder, etc.)
- Addictions (drugs, alcohol, porn, gambling, sex, tobacco, shopping, food, internet, gaming, etc.)

The list above is a few things to look for. However, this is not all that could go here; it serves as a guide to point you in the direction of things to look for. As you go through this book, you may want a journal handy to note issues you become aware of in your present situation. Identifying the problems that are present is part of the process of learning how to rid yourself of them. The book of Deuteronomy, chapter 28:15-68 describes a list of unfortunate outcomes associated with curses. These outcomes serve as indicators that a curse may be in effect, here are some that are not listed above:

- Living with emotional instability means constantly experiencing fear and confusion, which can affect every aspect of your life.

- Having a tendency to be unable to commit to plans, being frequently unreliable and flaky, and living without clear purpose or direction.

- Recurring, hereditary family illnesses refer to health issues that can be traced back to other family members and relatives, whether they are from the past or present. These health problems are inherited and can affect multiple generations within a family.

- Prone to frequent injuries, including lingering and chronic injuries, accidents, wounds, bruises, cuts, sores, and boils.

- Infertility can be a hereditary issue, affecting not just an individual but other family members as well.

This may manifest as barrenness, impotence, erectile dysfunction, and a range of female health issues, including unexplainable infections, hormone imbalances, menstrual problems, PMS, cramps, fibroids, painful intercourse, miscarriages, cysts, tumors, bladder problems, and kidney stones.

- Unusual marital problems can include significant delays in finding a suitable spouse, conflicts within the family, divorce, inclination towards having multiple spouses, difficulty in maintaining a stable marriage, frequently changing partners, a series of unexpected family crises, and dealing with rebellious children.

- Overpowering sexual immorality refers to the prevalence of behaviors such as incest, bestiality, addiction to pornography, sodomy (including lesbianism and homosexuality), and adulterous tendencies. This includes cases that involve other members of the family, whether in the past or present, further complicating the situation.

- The enduring impact of generational sins, including patterns of dishonesty, fraudulent behavior, alcoholism, and engaging in unhealthy sexual practices, poses a challenge for individuals who strive to break free from these destructive legacies.

- Experiencing unjustifiable financial hardship despite putting in significant effort at work, earning less than expected, and facing difficulty in generating wealth, as mentioned in Deuteronomy 28:17,29. Also, grappling with prolonged financial crisis without apparent reason, struggling to gain favor with others, and encountering repeated disappointments just as success seems within reach, Continuously exerting significant effort in the workplace and business dealings, yet not seeing corresponding results and frequently being taken advantage of. This situation leads to a lack of tangible progress despite consistent and diligent efforts.

- Debtorcracy, rooted in Deuteronomy 28:47-48, characterizes an individual becoming enslaved to borrowing and debt, finding it nearly impossible to break free from their financial burdens despite their efforts. This state also involves an inability to effectively manage and keep track of finances, leading to uncontrolled spending and wastage of resources before the individual realizes what is happening. Additionally, it encompasses being ensnared by get-rich-quick schemes and struggling with an addiction to them.

- Severe low self-esteem, as referenced in Deuteronomy 28:43-44, is frequently a consequence of enduring abuse, being overly indulged, experiencing betrayal, or living in fear. Individuals dealing with this may find that they have lost the freedom to express their true selves, struggle to make decisions independently, and constantly live in fear of speaking out. Even in cases of mistreatment and exploitation, they may continue to feel confined, akin to a caged individual.

- Some individuals are prone to being disliked by others without any apparent reason. They might frequently face punishment or blame for things they did not do.

If you feel something blocking your breakthrough, don't give up—there is hope.

Chapter Two

What is a generational curse?

What is a generational curse? A curse is the consequence of sinful behavior or wrongdoings. When left unchecked, our wrong actions or behaviors have repercussions. Think of it in terms of Isaac Newton's law on Action and Reaction. His third law states that for every action in nature, there is an equal and opposite reaction. This also applies to our behaviors. If we do good, we reap good. However, the reward for bad behavior works the same way. The Bible tells us in Galatians 6:7-9: "Do not be deceived; God is not mocked: for whatever a man sows, that he will also reap. For he who sows to his flesh will of the flesh reap corruption, but he who sows to the Spirit will of the Spirit reap life everlasting. And let us not be weary in well-doing, for in due season we shall reap if we do not faint." In other words, to reap good, you must end bad behavior or sinful nature.

The concept of sin was first introduced to us with Adam in the Garden of Eden. We learn of the immediate consequence of that first sin—a curse. It is often overlooked that this curse set in motion a pattern for future generations. In Genesis chapter 3, Eve sinned by disobeying God and eating the forbidden fruit. In verses 16-19, the consequences are described: "To the woman, he said, 'I will surely multiply your pain in childbearing; in pain, you shall bring forth children. Your desire shall be contrary to your husband, but he shall rule over you.' And to Adam, he said, 'Because you have listened to the voice of your wife and have eaten of the tree of which I commanded you, 'You shall not eat of it,' cursed is the ground because of you; in pain you shall eat of it all the days of your life; thorns and thistles it shall bring forth for you; and you shall eat the plants of the field. By the sweat of your face, you shall eat bread, till you return to the ground, for out of it you were taken; for you are dust, and to dust you shall return.'" This curse is the reason why we are all born with a sinful nature. If left unchecked, sin leads to destruction.

The father of sin uses every tactic he can to keep us bound in sin's trap. Jesus came to give us a way out of this prison. However, there are too many who think that he came to allow us to sin under grace. No, that is not what grace is for. Romans 6:1-2 reads, "What shall we say then? Shall we continue in sin, that grace may abound? God forbid. How shall we, that are dead to sin, live any longer therein?" Let us look at the information given as we revisit the question - what is a generational curse, and does it still apply to us today? A generational curse is the repercussion of sins passed down from generation to generation and left uncorrected. Look back at what we read in Galatians - to the one who repents and turns from his wicked ways, God forgives, and the sin curse is broken. But to the one who remains in sin, the curse remains.

Upon close examination, it becomes evident that the concept of a generational curse may not exist. Instead, it seems that it's the behavior that perpetuates the curse, NOT the curse itself being passed down. For instance, if Great Grandpa was an alcoholic, followed by Grandpa and then Dad, it's clear that the curse lies in the behavior. By continuing these actions, I would also inherit the curse. However, I have the power to break this cycle and spare my children and their children from this generational curse. I can choose to end the sin, thus breaking the curse. Nonetheless, identifying these sins is not always straightforward, as certain behaviors and traits are ingrained in us. We may even perceive them as normal because we've been told, "You know how this family is," or "It runs in the family." We should recognize that these statements signify a sin that leads to a curse. Our standard should be Jesus Christ; if the family's behaviors or attributes don't align with Him, it's a sin. If it contradicts the word of God, it's a sin. In God's eyes, there are no big or little sins—sin is sin, and they all carry the potential for a curse.

Breaking generational curses involves recognizing and actively addressing the destructive patterns and behaviors passed down through family lines. These harmful traits can manifest as anger, violence, manipulation, excessive criticism, and addictions, among others. It's important to acknowledge that these traits may not have originated with you but have been inherited from previous generations. These patterns not only affect your own well-being but also have a significant impact on your children and future descendants. By taking deliberate steps to understand and address these issues, you can break the cycle and prevent the continuation of these destructive patterns in future generations, paving the way for a healthier and more positive legacy for your family.

The subject of generational curses or any other curse is a controversial topic in the church world. Most people will not agree that it is possible for such things to happen. But yet, the Bible speaks about curses a lot. It is this disbelief that keeps people trapped in the bondage of curses. They refuse to take time to read the Bible for themselves and study it out. 1 Timothy 2:15 says, "Study to shew thyself approved unto God, a workman that needeth not to be ashamed, rightly dividing the word of truth." Don't fall for the trickery of what others believe. Know what you are fighting against and overcome. The behaviors you've learned have shaped the person you are today. You are a product of your environment, but that doesn't give you the right to transfer your pain onto others. It's time to start the healing process for yourself and your family. Blaming your past for your present issues is not the answer. The only way to break free is by acknowledging the chains that bind you. Jesus gave his life for our freedom from sin. It's time to identify and eliminate what is holding you back—your future generations are counting on it.

Before we move on, I want to highlight how I came to this revelation in my life. In 2022, I went to what I thought was just an average author convention. Every year, I attend a conference in Dahlonega. COVID was still rampant this year, and the meeting there was canceled. However, they informed us that one was being held the following month in Duluth. The invitation was highly recommended. So, the girls and I decided to attend. This conference was centered around Christian women writers. It was more of a weekend revival than an authors' meeting. It was phenomenal.

There was an author from California, and I'll repeat the woman at the well— "she told me everything I ever did." She told me things that she could only know through God. It was life-changing, to say the least. It was not the first time I had received a message stating that there was a curse on my bloodline. It was, however, the first time I decided to pray and ask for answers. The first time I had been told this was in 2017. Even then, I didn't know the person who had told me about the curse. But I would brush it off until this April weekend in 2022. I began to pray and ask God to reveal what these people were telling me. It has been a long process, but here I am now, sharing what I have learned on this journey. God showed me things all the way back to my childhood. I left home at the tender age of sixteen to get married. I wanted to be away from the people who were hurting me, not in my home, but in my family. I thought that if I were married, then I wouldn't have to be around these people. However, being so young, I didn't realize that I couldn't run from the damage done by these terrible things. I thought I was running away, but in reality, I was running straight into the repercussions of the curse. I hadn't dealt with it—I hadn't faced it or spoken out about it—so it attached itself to me. It followed and dictated my life for many years.

Because of the curse, I moved away once I had children. I was trying to protect them from the people who had hurt me. They only saw their grandparents once or twice a year. Because of the curse, they were denied access to people they loved and who loved them. Even upon moving back, they were hurt by people who spoke badly of them—Because of the curse. Then God dealt with me about writing this book. I pray that it can shorten the course of chaos for someone else. Acknowledge it, call it out, and renounce it. Then you can be free from it. Sometimes, being free means, you must distance yourself from those who remain under the curse. You can't free those who don't want to be free, but you can walk away if that is what it takes to be free.

Chapter Three

Religion or Righteousness

Now that you have examined your life and noted undesirable traits and behaviors in your family line, let's begin by looking at the essential key to ridding your life of curses.

On this journey, God had me digging deep into my family history. At the beginning, I didn't know where to begin. I didn't even know what I was looking for. What stuck out the most was how my family's beliefs changed through the years. I do want to emphasize that I am in no way bashing denominations on churches. I only wish to point out that God did not create denominations—man did.

Let me give you a brief example of my family, and I will explain it further.

My 6th great-grandfather, Christopher Pless, arrived in America in 1751 on Ship Ann in South Carolina. He was 16 years old. They were German Lutheran. In 1789, Christopher helped build the Organ Zion Lutheran Church in Salisbury, North Carolina. He and one of his sons, Henry, are buried there. His son Philip is my 5th great-grandfather. Philip and his son Abraham's religious affiliations are unknown. We only know that they are buried somewhere in Georgia. However, my 3rd and 2nd great-grandfathers, Seaborn and James William, were Baptist, and they are buried in Gainesville, Georgia. John Monroe and my grandfather are where we start to see the denomination change to what I was raised in—Holiness. Being tired of denominational discrepancies, in the early part of the 2000s, my dad, Sonny, would go Independent.

Why is this important? Jeremiah 6:16 says, "Thus saith the Lord, stand ye in the ways and seek and ask for the old paths, where is the good way, and walk therein, and ye shall find rest for your souls. But they said we will not walk therein." That last statement is most people's problem. They don't want to live according to God's word.

They search out denominations that fit their lifestyles instead of the truth of what the Bible tells us. People quote partial verses that they think excuse them to sin. "The spirit is willing, but the flesh is weak," they say. Let us look at the verse in its entirety. Matthew 26:41, "Watch and pray, that ye enter not into temptation: the spirit is willing, but the flesh is weak." This is why knowing the Bible for yourself is crucial. Jesus is saying here that because the flesh is weak, you must watch and pray so you don't fall into temptation or sin.

For most of my life, my dad was a pastor. He was raised in the holiness faith and preached according to their beliefs. However, throughout the years, he would get in the car on the way home and say to my mom, "Something just isn't adding up." Or "I don't understand, according to their beliefs, that shouldn't be happening." When he brought this question up to some of the people of the church or in his family he was met with opposition. So, he would let it go. A few years went by, and he had to resign from the church to care for my mom. It was during this time that he really studied the Bible and prayed for a deeper understanding. He started to realize that some of the things they were teaching went against what the Bible was saying.

God does not put a dress code on people; the Bible says, "adorn themselves in modest apparel." (1 Timothy 2:9); this does not mean women have to wear dresses all the time. Nor do men have to wear a suit and tie to preach. This limits salvation to people who can afford to dress to code. Please understand that this is man's rules, not God's. Baptism is another touchy subject. According to the Bible, it should be performed according to Acts 2:38. It is in Acts that the writer begins to teach us how to act under the new covenant. But just as Luke, Peter, Paul and the others met with opposition back then, it is still occurring today. People want to stick with what they have always been taught instead of searching it out for themselves.

Growing up in this family, I've heard many people refer to us as being a "religious" people. History proves this seems to be correct. However, the Pharisees in the Bible were a religious people, and they crucified Jesus. Religious people are best described by 1 Timothy 3:5-7, "Having a form of godliness but denying the power thereof: from such turn away. For of this sort they which creep into houses, and lead captive silly women laden with sin, led away with divers lusts. Ever learning and never able to come to the knowledge of the truth."

Yes, I agree there are a lot of religious people in my family; they are always learning but never accepting the truth. But we are not all religious; there are a few righteous people. Righteousness is what you want to seek. "He that followeth after righteousness and mercy findeth life, righteousness, and honor"—Proverbs 21:21. "The eyes of the Lord are upon the righteous, and his ears are open unto their cry"—Psalm 34:15. And lastly, one of my favorites, "For he that will love life, and see good days, let him refrain his tongue from evil, and his lips that they speak no guile: Let him eschew evil, and do good, let him seek peace, and ensue it. For the eyes of the Lord are over the righteous, and his ears are open to their prayers: but the face of the Lord is against them that do evil. And who is he that will harm you, if ye be followers of that which is good? But and if ye suffer the righteousness' sake, happy are ye: and be not afraid of their terror neither be troubled but sanctify the Lord God in your hearts: and be ready always to give an answer to every man that asketh you a reason of the hope that is in you with meekness and fear"—1 Peter 3:10-15.

Seeking God's righteousness is the first step in ending curses. You must come to Jesus, repent of your sins, seek out the old paths of truth, and walk in them. As long as the sin is there, so is the curse. Being disobedient to Christ is also a sin. 1 Samuel 15:23 tells us this, "For rebellion is as the sin of witchcraft, and stubbornness is as iniquity and idolatry. Because thou hast rejected the word of the Lord, he hath also rejected thee from being king." We are rebellious or disobedient when we try to change the word of God to fit us or refuse to live, preach, or teach it the way it is written. Stubbornness—ah, now there's a word you will also hear people say when describing my family. It is stubbornness that keeps them from accepting the truth and turning from "What we've always been taught." They'd rather believe a lie and be damned than accept the truth. 2 Thessalonians 2:10-12, "And with all deceivableness of unrighteousness in them that perish; because they received not the love of the truth, that they might be saved; and for this cause God shall send them strong delusion, that they should believe a lie: that they all might be damned who believe not the truth but had pleasure in unrighteousness."

The only way to know the truth is to read it for yourself. Never take someone else's word for the truth without searching it out for yourself. Not even me. I want you to let this book encourage you to get into the Bible and search out these things I'm writing, read them, and study them. You have two choices: You can seek religion, find one that fits your lifestyle, walk in the form of godliness, and deny the power thereof. However, the curse remains. Or you can turn from sin that has been handed down, seek out the true path of righteousness, and free yourself from the curse of that sin. Then, the next time someone says, "I know how your family is," You can say, "I belong to the family of Jesus Christ; I don't identify with that crowd anymore." The choice is yours.

To wrap up this chapter, I want to explain that my examples are not the only misunderstandings out there. You are looking for anything that goes against Biblical teaching, including abusive behavior of any kind, bullying people, and overusing authority towards coworkers, family, friends, or even your children, such as name-calling, degrading, making fun of people, condoning bad behavior by not speaking up, or spreading rumors. And yet, still, this is not the complete list. As you study the Bible and develop a sincere prayer life, God will reveal what needs to be fixed. Don't hold on to beliefs just because that is what grandpa did, or daddy did—search it out for yourself. Don't let stubbornness keep you out of Heaven. It's not worth it. I wasted so many years caught up in a thinking cycle that held me captive, and I would have loved it if someone had given me this knowledge years ago. It has made a huge difference in my life, and God has permitted me to share it with you. Take notes as you go along, let this information transform your life. Take it back to God.

Chapter Four

The Silence Ends Here

Have you noticed any mistreatment in your family? Maybe family secrets of cruel or destructive behaviors towards others? This is another area that God started showing me where my own family brought curses into the bloodline. This chapter comes with a trigger warning if reading about acts of violence upsets you. This book is titled Breaking the Silence because that is what you must do to end this type of curse. However, I also want to point out that under no circumstance am I trying to shame anyone. That is why names are withheld when needed. This is not about calling people out individually; it's about calling out the sins that have been handed down. The stories I share are my own experiences in my life, making them my story to tell. I refuse to live another day under the sinful curses of my family bloodline. It's time to break the silence and free myself and generations beyond me of the same sins and curses.

As I was doing my research, I began to see a pattern in certain behaviors. However, the one that nauseated me the most was the sins committed against children. I was one of those children, but I'm not the only one, and it continues today with some. As a matter of fact, it had happened long before me. Remember me mentioning that Grandpa did it; Daddy did it; now it's my turn at the beginning of the book. This is one of those situations. It's no surprise that there are so many people having fertility problems, miscarriages, and even infant deaths in my family. The things I've heard, read, and experienced are beyond disturbing. We'll start with disappearing parents.

We have worked for months now, almost a year, and yet we still can't get past some of the dead ends. This isn't just on one side of the tree; it's on all trees. We have found some notations left behind that explain that some fathers refuse to recognize their responsibility as parents, and the children were never legitimized. We found men who had children with multiple women with children around the same ages on each side. Although I could give many examples of this, I'll use the one that is public knowledge: a great uncle, James Daniel Davis. James was working out of town; he had an affair. Upon finding out about the pregnancy, he informed the young lady that he was already married and had children back home. Although he had nine children with his first wife, he went to Gainesville, Georgia, with his sister Hannah (my great-grandmother). He would then go on with his life and pretend the child didn't exist. Hannah, however, would keep in contact with the child. He would eventually marry another woman in North Carolina but leave before their son was born. He would go back to Georgia to live with a daughter from his first wife, and this is where he died three years after arriving there. This story gives a good visual for what I mean by disappearing parents and children who were never legitimized.

In these situations, the blame doesn't just rest on the fathers; the mothers are also held accountable. Even when a marriage ends with divorce, both parents are responsible for making sure those children are well provided for, and their mental and physical situations are well maintained.

Being severed from the relationship gives neither parent a free card to disappear from the children's lives or their care. The example above happened a few generations back. However, I have seen this in recent years. My children's dad hasn't been part of their life since they were three and four. So, I've seen firsthand what this does to a child. Another way I've seen this abuse take place is with parents who are physically with their children but not properly attending to their well-being. Neglecting a child is wrong no matter what the situation is.

Before going on, I think this would be an excellent point to put what the Bible says about children and parents. Mark 10:13-14 says, "and they were bringing children to him that he might touch them, and the disciples rebuked them. But when Jesus saw it, he was indignant and said to them, "let the children come to me; do not hinder them, for such belongs the kingdom of God. Truly, I say to you, whoever does not receive the kingdom of God like a child shall not enter it." And he took them in his arms and blessed them, laying his hands on them." Then we have Ephesians 6:4, "Fathers, do not provoke your children to anger, but bring them up in the discipline and instruction of the Lord." Galatians 3:21: "Fathers, do not provoke your children, lest they become discouraged." And then, Proverbs 22:6 says this, "Train up a child in the way that he should go; even when he is old, he will not depart from it."

It is abundantly clear what the Bible teaches about the issue of child abuse of any kind. Child abuse in any form is evil. It doesn't matter if it's my family or someone else's. If you are abusing a child, you are not only sinning, but you are also bringing anger and hurt to that child; you are planting a seed for that child to do the same sins you are committing, and where the sin seed grows—so does the curse. What kind of example are we setting for our children? Before moving on, that question needs serious thought and answered honestly. Because this next sin is more disturbing than abandoning them— Sexual abuse against a child.

My parents didn't abandon me. I was raised in a Christian home, and if there's one thing I can say of my parents, they did everything in their power to protect us. However, this sin is a harsh reality of my childhood. In my book, The Long Road Home, I tell the story of how I was sexually assaulted at six years old by an uncle. This wasn't the first time this uncle had molested me, only this time, he was more aggressive with his actions, and I was physically hurt. I can also add that some other uncles and cousins did the same. This is a big sin that must stop in my family! It goes on beyond child molestation—it continues even as an adult. There are men in my family that I will not let in my house when I'm alone, nor allow myself to be alone with anywhere. The Bible speaks powerfully against sexual sin. Sex is a gift given by God meant for marriage. Sexual perversion of all kinds is soundly condemned. Sexually assaulting a child is never justifiable; it is always wrong.

Now, let's look at the flip side of this coin. Anyone who suspects that a child is being abused is obligated to speak up for that child and protect it. Even if this means someone else you love goes to jail or is punished by law. To force sexual acts upon a child is a horrible, evil offense. In addition to committing a sexual sin, the perpetrator is also attacking the innocence of one of the world's most vulnerable persons. Sexual abuse violates everything about a person, from their understanding of self to physical boundaries to spiritual connection with God. In a child, these things are so barely established that they are often altered for life and, without appropriate help, may not ever heal. So, why would you choose not to stand up for that child and protect it? Why would you protect the freedom and reputation of the perpetrator who did this to them? Do you not know that the Bible tells us to protect and look after others? James 1:27 says that caring for children in need pleases God: "Religion that God our Father accepts as pure and faultless is this: to look after orphans and widows in their distress and to keep oneself from being polluted by the world." Followers of Christ are consistently called to love others. Molesting a child can in no way be mistaken for love. Proverbs 31:8-9 says, "Open your mouth for the mute, for the rights of all who are destitute. Open your mouth, judge righteously, defend the rights of the poor and needy." It does not say to keep quiet or protect the evil one—this is saying to stand up for the ones who can't stand up for themselves.

Children are abused and mistreated in several ways, all of which are abhorrent to God. The Bible prohibits child abuse in its warnings against improper anger. Too many children are the victims of angry beatings and other physical abuse as their parents take out their anger and frustration on their children. Though some forms of physical discipline may be biblically acceptable, such discipline should never be administered in anger. Paul reminds the Ephesians, "In your anger do not sin: Do not let the sun go down while you are still angry and do not give the devil a foothold" (Ephesians 4:26-27). Proverbs 29:22 says, "An angry man stirs up dissension, and a hot-tempered one commits many sins." There is no place for unrighteous or uncontrolled anger in the life of a Christian. Anger should be confessed to God and appropriately handled long before it comes to the point of physical abuse against a child or anyone else. Another way the Bible prohibits child abuse is in its forbidding of psychological and emotional abuse. Ephesians 6:4 warns fathers not to "exasperate" or provoke their children but to bring them up in the "training and instruction of the Lord." Harsh, unloving verbal discipline, emotional manipulation, or volatile environments alienate children's minds from their parents and render their instruction and correction useless. Parents can provoke and exasperate their children by placing unreasonable requirements on them, belittling them, or constantly finding fault, thereby producing wounds that can be as bad as or worse than any physical beating can inflict. Colossians 3:21 tells us not to "embitter" our children so they will not become discouraged. Ephesians 4:15-19 says we are to speak the truth in love and use our words to build others up, not allow rotten or destructive words to pour from our lips, especially towards the tender hearts and minds of children.

If you or someone you know is being molested, or you suspect abuse, you must contact the appropriate authorities. If you were abused as a child and suspect that your abuser is still harming others—you must report it—speak up! Looking the other way or blaming the child or adult that is being abused is wrong! The one thing I hate the most is being told as a child that I had to keep the abuse to myself, or I'd get in trouble because they'd think it was my fault or that I lied and that my parents would get in trouble, or they'd harm my parents if I told them. The perpetrator didn't just tell me this; I was told this the one time I dared to tell another adult. Being a child, I believed this. I learned that in my family, people just look the other way and keep their mouths shut when someone is hurting or bullying others. We are wrong for that behavior. We are just as guilty as the ones with the abusive behavior. The Bible calls us to be "peacemakers," Matthew 5:9 says, "Blessed are the peacemakers: for they shall be called the children of God." And remember Proverbs 31:9, "Open thy mouth, judge righteously, and plead the cause of the poor and needy."

I am in no way innocent of any wrongdoing here. I've had to apologize for not speaking up when I should have. I'm not the only one in my family to whom this has happened. Others have come forward and shared their stories, too. The uncle that hurt me—also hurt others. And would go on to hurt his child, too. The curse stops here for me—it stops here in my bloodline! It can stop in yours, too. If you are the one doing the harm, stop now. Give it to Jesus and let him guide you in the way to ask forgiveness for what you have done to people. Make right the best you can what you have bestowed upon others. Believe me when I say that it helps to hear a sincere apology from the ones who admit they were wrong for hurting you. I've never got that from the ones that hurt me. Take time to right your wrongs with those you've harmed in any way. The Bible tells us how to fix these issues: Confess (James 5:16), Correct (Matthew 18:15), draw in other believers, if necessary (Matthew 18:16), Repent (Acts 8:22), Forgive (Mark 11:25), Be reconciled (Matthew 5:13-24), Strive hard to live in harmony (Romans 12:16; 1 Corinthians 1:10). These steps also help the ones who have been abused. Did you know that if you don't forgive someone who has wronged you, Christ won't forgive you? Matthew 6:14-15 says that God will not forgive a person who doesn't forgive others. In the verse, Jesus states: "For if you forgive other people when they sin against you, your heavenly Father will also forgive you. But if you do not forgive others their sins, your Father will not forgive your sins."

To wrap up this chapter, I want to repeat that I am not writing this to shame or call out people. As I mentioned before, I've had to apologize to people that I could have protected if only I had spoken up. There were times when I could have stepped in when I noticed that children weren't being properly cared for. I had heard some say, "It doesn't matter what you say in this family. They are always going to protect the bad ones." This is true, and people have done and said these things. But that doesn't justify the actions that I should have taken and did nothing. I've also heard that if you report them, then someone else is hurt—the mom whose child is punished by law—the children whose parent is locked away. It's this thinking that keeps the sin being passed down, and therefore, the curse remains on everyone involved. It's time we all Break the Silence. In my ministry I work with a lot of people, primarily women, that are dealing with this issue. This seems to be a big problem in the world today. However, it is not something that has just started happening. It's happening because no one will stand up and stop it. Be the voice of a child today. Let's put an end to this curse once and for all. It's our responsibility as Christians to protect the ones who can't protect themselves. If we are standing by and doing nothing, we are letting Satan have the upper hand in destroying our children at a young age. Stand up, speak out, shout it loud—the silence ends here.

Here are some more Bible verses on the raising of children for you to read and study:

- Proverbs 22:6—Train up a child in the way he should go; even when he is old, he will not depart from it.

- Deuteronomy 4:40—Therefore you shall keep his statutes and his commandments, which I command you today, that it may go well with you and with your children after you, and that you may prolong your days in the land that the Lord you god is giving you for all time.

- Proverbs 15:4—Discipline your son while there is hope and do not desire his death.

- Titus 2:7-8—In everything, set them an example by doing what is good. In your teaching, show integrity, seriousness, and soundness of speech that cannot be condemned so that those who oppose you may be ashamed because they have nothing bad to say about us.

- Proverbs 17:6—Children's children are a crown to the aged, and parents are the pride of their children.

- Psalm 127:3—Behold, children are a heritage from the Lord, the fruit of the womb a reward.

- Deuteronomy 11:18-19—You shall therefore lay up these words of mine in your heart and in your soul, and you shall bind them as a sign on your hand, and they shall be as frontlets between your eyes. You shall teach them to your Children, talking of them when you are sitting in your house, and when you are walking by the way, and when you lie down, and when you rise.

- Colossians 3:20—Children, obey your parents in everything for this pleases the Lord.

This last one is important too. How we treat our parents also can result in our blessings being taken away and replaced with a curse. Exodus 20:12 says, "Honor your father and mother, that your days may be long in the land that the Lord your God is giving you." You may not like what they do or how they act, but you do have to honor them as the ones who birthed you. You still have to love them—even if it's from a distance.

Chapter Five

No Bullying Allowed

Scroll through any social media, and you will probably run across a post with a mom fuming with rage over their child being bullied at school. Ever wonder where children learn this behavior? Research is firm in its belief that children learn what they live. Most often, a child who is bullied at school is being bullied or sees someone else being bullied at home. Sometimes, this behavior at home can also have the reverse effect of allowing this child to be bullied at school. Either way, the child's life is affected by what they live in at home. In this chapter, we will be looking at what the Bible tells us about this type of behavior and how it can tie us to a sin curse if not broken.

Let us start with an example of this behavior. In my family, I had an uncle with a bad reputation for harming and bullying people. The stories that floated around were that he had worked anonymously to—let's just say—clean up problems for someone. He used this to his advantage with everyone, throwing his weight around as if he were untouchable. I am not sure if he bullied his children and wife, but I know he bullied his brothers, sisters, nieces, and nephews. Most likely, the people in his house were bullied, too. Before going forward, I do want to say that he was not the only bully in the family, just the worst one. Most everyone was intimidated by him—but not all. He loved to sit around and proudly talk on his excursion as if he deserved a medal for what he had done to people. After all, most of these people were rumored to be bad people. He thought that telling these stories gave him power over everyone. But that wasn't always the case. There was this one story told about him approaching a niece about a piece of furniture he wanted. He told her that if he wanted it, he'd just take it. She challenged him to try and see what happened. This uncle then asked her if she knew who she was dealing with and if she knew that he always gets his way. She stood her ground and told him—not this time. He never got the piece of furniture he wanted.

Most people around the area where I live know the reputation tacked onto my family. They say, "They are nice people until you cross them, then they are mean." Or "They are a very religious family—but you have to watch them; they can be mean and vindictive." These are quotes that people have said to me directly about my family. We even have a few who were known to be untrustworthy. There is one uncle that most would tell you not to believe anything he told you. Then there are those that you best not buy what they are selling because it's probably not theirs. Let's not forget the numerous uncles, aunts, and cousins that you should never trust to be alone with your wives, husbands, or children. Remember me mentioning that there are male family members that I will not allow in my home if I am there alone? That last statement is why. They have no respect for their own family. This also goes for the women. There are women in this family—born and married into it—that can't be trusted around others alone. I've heard so many stories from others that time will not allow me to write examples on everything, but I will say this—if the other person goes along with said behaviors and does not tell their spouse or parent (talking about adults here), they are just as guilty as the ones pursuing this behavior. If my dad's brothers or nephews solicited my mom—she should have gone to my dad about this issue, not go along with it. When I say it doesn't matter who is doing the wrong—it doesn't matter who is doing the wrong—it needs to end.

Although the word bullying is not used in the Bible, we do find the word brutish, a synonym for the brutal thuggery associated with thieves, assassins, and savage beasts. The Hebrew and Greek words translated as "brute" or "brutish" mean—stupid, foolish, and irrational, as cattle. We can derive from this that those who bully are acting like cattle or another beast incapable of rational thought. The Bible may not speak specifically about bullies or bullying but many biblical principles apply to the issue. First, it is crucial to understand what bullying is. A simple definition would be using superior strength or power to intimidate people. Bullies are those who prey on people they perceive as weak and threaten them with harm, or actually harm them, to get their way. Obviously, bullying is not godly. Christians are called to love others and look out for those who are weaker, not intimidate or manipulate people. James 1:27 states: "Religion that is pure and undefiled before God the Father is this: to visit orphans and widows in their affliction, and to keep oneself unstained from the world." Then we have 1 John 3:17-18, "But if anyone has the world's goods and sees his brother in need, yet closes his heart against him, how does God's love abide in him? Little children, let us not love in word or talk but in deed and in truth." Finally, Galatians 6:9-10 says, "And let us not grow weary of doing good, for in due season we will reap if we do not give up. To them, as we have the opportunity, let us do good to everyone, and especially to those who are of the household of faith." These verses let us know that it is evident that Christians should not be bullies.

Generally, there are two situations in which a Christian may need to respond to bullying: when he is the victim of bullying and when he is a witness to bullying. When being bullied, the proper response might be turning the other cheek, or it might be self-defense. When Jesus spoke of turning the other cheek in Matthew 5:38-42, he taught us to refrain from retaliating to personal slights. The idea is not to return an insult with an insult. When someone verbally abuses us, we do not return his affront with insults of our own. When someone tries to assert his position of power to intimidate us or force us into a particular behavior, we can resist his manipulation without being manipulative in return. In short, bullying a bully is not biblical and, quite frankly, not practical. It is, however, advisable to report the bullying to the proper authorities. It is not wrong for a person to report a con artist to the police. Such actions may help prevent the bully from harming others. Even when we do not retaliate on a personal level, we can still utilize social systems of justice. When bullying is physical, self-defense may be appropriate. The Bible does not advocate total pacifism. God's instructions to Israel in Exodus 22 and Jesus' instructions to his disciples to get a sword in Luke 22 are informative. Christians are to be loving and forgiving but not permissive of evil.

When a Christian observes bullying, it is appropriate to intervene and help prevent the attack against the victim. Each situation will be different, and many times, intervening will add to the problem, but often, it takes just one person to stand up on behalf of a weaker party to stop the bullying and prevent it in the future. However, we never victimize the victim. This happens so often. "It must have somehow been their fault." Or we try to make excuses for the bully because he or she is someone close to us. It is not godly to condone bad behavior. The Bible tells us not to be partakers in another man's sin (1

Timothy 5:22-24). As Christians, we need to pray for those who treat others cruelly. However, we need to report when necessary if the behavior puts people in danger of physical harm. Thieves should be reported, too, along with drug dealers and anyone else breaking the law. When we don't report these things, we are taking part in their wrongdoings. We are not standing up for the weak and the defenseless. Think of all the young kids dying daily from drug use, and you know of a drug dealer who is putting it on the streets for them.

I remember a story from my childhood that used to disturb me. It was about a great-uncle who got into a fight with a man and ended up shooting and killing him. The unsettling part was that he then placed the man on the bed and slept beside him until calling the police in the morning. Despite being taken to jail, he was never booked or tried for the crime. It's puzzling how our family seemed to have connections with law enforcement in that town, allowing him to escape justice. Later on, another family member was also rumored to have committed crimes and got away with them due to the family's influence in the town. It is this kind of sinful behavior that puts curses on a bloodline. How? Because this behavior and attitude is still being passed down. There are some in the younger generation that still maintain this attitude. Bullying and thinking they are untouchable. The other side of this is people who know about this and are doing nothing to stop it; remember, in chapter four, we talked about knowing about wrongs and sitting back and not intervening; this applies here, too. Bullying, soliciting sexual practices with family members or those married into the family, being dishonest, stealing, drugging and selling drugs, or any form of dishonest lifestyle. If you practice these behaviors, it needs to stop; if you condone, protect, or lie for the ones who do this—that too needs to stop. I'll repeat it one more time—if the sin continues, so does the curse.

Family Secrets is the place to start to understand this section better. They are usually the stories that are handed down from generation to generation. Think about those, and you will probably start to see, as I did, that something is very off with them. However, there are those secrets that you may only hear bits and pieces of and never enough details to know exactly what happened. But it is these things that keep us bound to a curse. We are raised in an environment that teaches us that this is just how it is in our family—this is just who we are. Stand with me today and say—not me! Repent of any wrongs you've done or condoned, read your Bible, apply it to your life, and come into a new family of Christ and free yourself of that curse.

Bible verses to study:

- Titus 3:1-5—Put them in mind to be subject to principalities and powers, and obey magistrates, to be ready to every good work, to speak evil of no man, to be no brawlers, but gentle, showing all meekness unto all men. For we ourselves also were sometimes foolish, disobedient, deceived, serving divers lusts and pleasures, living in malice and envy, hateful, and hating one another. But after that, the kindness and love of God our Saviour toward man appeared, Not by works of righteousness which we have done, but according to his mercy he saved us, by the washing of regeneration, and renewing of the Holy Ghost;

- Ephesians 4:28-32—Let him that stole steal no more: but rather let him labor, working with his hands the thing which is good, that he may have to have to him that needeth. Let no corrupt communication proceed out of your mouth, but that which is good the use of edifying, that it may minister grace unto the hearers. And grieve not the holy Spirit of God, whereby ye are sealed unto the day of redemption. Let bitterness, and wrath, and anger, and clamour, and evil speaking, be put away from you, with all malice: And be ye kind one to another, tenderhearted, forgiving one another, even as God for Christ's sake hath forgiven you.

I have a story to share about the profound effects of bullying, particularly on young people. During my daughter's preteen years, she faced bullying from relatives at church. She struggled with health issues that led to weight problems and a weak bladder, and these relatives ruthlessly mocked her for these challenges, as well as for her singing and the way she laughed. When she was 15, a routine check-up at the doctor's office revealed something alarming. My daughter couldn't bear to remove her jacket and broke down in tears, revealing that she had been engaging in self-harm as a result of the emotional trauma caused by the bullying. It was a heartbreaking realization that led us to distance ourselves from these individuals who were unable to show love and empathy. This experience served as a powerful reminder of the importance of considering the impact of our words and actions before teasing or mocking others.

Usually, the people who choose this type of bullying have issues within themselves. Why would people who are confident in who God created them to be have a desire to hurt or degrade others? It was this type of bullying that could have caused me to lose my child. Some people have lost loved ones because of this. Don't be the reason that someone chooses not to live anymore. As Christians, we are called to love the way Christ loves us. He would never humiliate people. Jesus is the only one who can rid a person of this kind of behavior. People who hurt people are usually hurt people. These are people who have not dealt with the curses in their own lives. Therefore, they convey this hurt to others. When we know who Christ is and who He really created us to be, we can then mend ourselves to lift others up and not try to tear them down for having courage and strength that we don't have. I don't feel intimidated by people who are higher up than I am—I want to learn from them so that I, too, can rise. But people who haven't come to the knowledge of the truth don't like it when someone is doing better than them. It is at that point that they set out to tear down what others have built. And it is so easy to get caught in this destructive pattern if you are not rooted in Christ daily. The sadness in this is—it is not strangers that do this; these are people we know and love, and that's how it hurts us so much. These are people who should be supporting us in our journey, but instead, they see us as a threat to their insufficiency. Love from a distance if you must. Don't let them hinder your growth in Christ.

Chapter Six

Tying It All Together

As we advance, we will discuss curses from a different angle. In this chapter, we will review what we have discussed already and give more insight into understanding what a curse is and how to free yourself of these ties that keep us bound and hold us back from God. The sins we have discussed so far are just a glimpse into how deep this really goes. Think about everything you hear people say, 'It runs in the family' about. It is these destructive behaviors and illnesses or traits that you need to get to the core of. The only way it can be handed down is if the behavior behind it is also handed down. Ever notice that when you go to the doctor's office, the first thing they do is, have you fill out a form on family history? If they were honest with you, they would be an excellent place to start because they know exactly what causes each of those illnesses that run in your family. And many are a sin.

Let's start by naming a few health issues: overweight, joint pain, heart disease, type 2 diabetes, gastroesophageal reflux disease (GERD), poor nutrition, cancer, high blood pressure, and some sleep-related breathing disorders. The cause of all of this? Overeating. What does the Bible say about overeating? In Proverbs 23:1-3, it is written: "When you sit to eat with a ruler, consider diligently what is before thee, and put a knife to your throat if you are given to appetite. Be not desirous of his dainties: for they are deceitful meat." This means that when we overeat, we are harming ourselves, inviting preventable diseases. The mention of "dainties" refers to sweets, delicacies, and confections, which are especially harmful to our health. Many families struggle with this, as we often turn to food as a comfort in difficult times or as a means of celebration. Stress and unhealthy coping mechanisms are closely related. Jesus encourages us to give our worries to him in Matthew 11, reminding us that his yoke is easy and his burden is light. When we try to handle things on our own, we often end up stressed about issues that are not meant for us to carry. This includes bearing family secrets, which can cause a significant emotional burden. These behaviors are learned and not what we were meant to indulge in, especially after finding the truth.

In this first part of the book, we have been looking at behaviors we have control over. These are behaviors that we were taught by those before us. We started with what we have been taught about biblical beliefs and how some people add to and take away from the word of God to adapt it to fit their lives. Some even use scripture out of context. We read about a few of those in chapter three. But there are others as well. Nowhere in the Bible does it condone someone being abused. Nor does it permit men to treat their wives as if they are children. Jesus freed everyone from bondage—not just the men. The Bible doesn't say a woman can't work. The beloved Proverbs 31 women worked. Read it carefully. However, that job can't come before a woman's duty at home. The needs of the home and her family need to be always met. This also applies to the men. Work can't come before God and the family.

When we marry someone, we become one with that person, and we are to pray for and encourage each other in Christ. Ephesians 5:25 says, "Wives, submit yourselves unto your own husbands, as unto the Lord. For the husband is the head of the wife, even as Christ is the head of the church: and he is the Savior of the body. Therefore, as the church is subject unto Christ, so let the wives be to their own husbands in everything. Husbands love your wives, even as Christ also loved the church and gave himself for it."

The above verse tells the wives to submit to their husbands. This means that a wife should respect her husband, and it does not give the husband permission to belittle his wife and treat her like a child. Submission in a marriage is not reticence, servanthood, inferiority, docile, degrading, and not a sign of weakness. In fact, submission in marriage is a sign of strength, not of weakness. It requires a great degree of personal strength of character. This does not mean that a man dominates and always gets his way. A wife practicing submission to her husband does not mean she should be a silent "yes" person or a doormat. Nor does it mean she should have no opinion of her own. Rather, a wife who chooses to take an attitude of submission towards her husband is a wife who has a heart of being supportive of her husband. In choosing to support her husband, she empowers him to have the self-respect he needs. He will develop into the kind of man who accepts his role and responsibilities in the home. He will seek to fulfill his God-ordained position of protecting, providing for, and leading his family. When a wife submits, she is a helper to her husband in the broad, biblical sense. In other words—submitting means working with each other and not against each other.

When a husband demonstrates a heart of submission in marriage, his wife is a pleasure to be around. The husband appreciates and admires her because she is one he can trust. As a result, he can feel at peace and content. He can trust her with his deepest desires and fears because he is not afraid of her scorning, competing, or rejecting him. He can relax with her because he knows that even when he makes mistakes, she will work with him to help him correct them. The husband can feel secure in himself that she will be working to minimize the consequence of his mistake rather than trying to prove a point or reject him in some way.

Biblical submission in marriage is a wife making a choice not to overtly resist her husband's will. That is not to say that she cannot disagree with him or that she cannot express her opinion. Indeed, a wife who practices submission is, by definition, a woman with the strength of character. She will, therefore, usually have her own opinions and ideas about issues. These may often be different from the opinions of her husband. However, she can express her opinions and ideas respectfully without belittling and without disrespectful confrontation. It might sometimes be wrong for her not to express her opinion. She is ordained by God to be her husband's helper, not his doormat. By expressing her opinions, giving advice, and offering suggestions, she will be an invaluable partner to her husband.

To sum this up—men, she is a helpmate, not a slave to you. She belongs to God, not you. God only loaned her to you to help you in life's journey. Women you are free to live life as needed. Your husband's permission to make a grocery run is not required. A controlling husband who uses this verse to say you are sinning if you go against his wishes—He is the one sinning. He is misinterpreting this verse for his own selfish, insecure reasons. However, don't disrespect him; instead, kindly let him know that he has no reason not to trust you. The man (or woman) who tries to control people usually has trust issues, and many men misinterpret the Bible to control women. As I said above— Jesus freed all from bondage, and he doesn't intend for any of us to live under bondage to anyone.

You can't take verses of the Bible out of context and put them to mean whatever suits you. That is what is done with this scripture and many others. We are told to rightfully divide the word of truth. This verse says, "Study to shew thyself approved unto God, a workman that needeth not to be ashamed, rightly dividing the word of truth. But shun profane and vain babblings: for they will increase unto the more ungodliness. (1 Timothy 15-16)." This verse emphasizes the importance of diligent study and accurate interpretation of Scripture. No verse is going to contradict another. Matthew 7:12 tells us to "do for others what you would want them to do for you. This is the meaning of the Law of Moses and the teachings of the prophets." This goes for husbands and wives also. Then we have Philippians 2:3-5, "Let nothing be done through strife and vainglory, but in lowliness of mind let each esteem other better than themselves. Look not every man on his own thing, but every man also on the things of others. Let this mind be in you, which was also in Christ Jesus." Child of God—study to show thyself approved, don't take verses out of context. Don't do something just because it was handed down through the generational grapevine—search out the truth and be free from the bondage and curse of sin.

Knowing what the Bible tells us about how to treat people and putting that into action in our lives covers most of the sins that we have discussed so far in the book. Remember that we are told in 1 Peter 3:17-18, "Ye therefore, beloved, seeing ye know these things before, beware lest ye also, being led away with the error of the wicked, fall from your own steadfastness. But grow in grace and in the knowledge of our Lord and Savior Jesus Christ. To him be glory both now and forever. Amen." We are told to grow in the grace/favor and knowledge of our Lord Jesus Christ. One of the things we must learn to do when it comes to acquiring knowledge is to be willing to unlearn previously held beliefs when clear scripture shows us the correct doctrine or teaching. We all must do this. I continue to learn more about God and the written word every day and continue to have to discard old ideas that I see now were just plain wrong. Perhaps you were raised in a racist home, and you now realize that Christ came and died for their sins too, that Christ loves them too—and when he speaks of loving all of mankind—he's speaking of loving them too. So now we must unlearn the idea that taught us that God only loves those who fit a certain demographic. Then, we replace them with what's true, but fully unlearning is really hard sometimes. It can be exciting when God reveals a truth in the Bible that contradicts what you previously believed. However, it can also be challenging because it raises the question of how to approach the people who taught you the untruth. What if they are unwilling to accept the truth? What if it leads to being disconnected from family? This is because sometimes people's pride prevents them from admitting that they were wrong.

This is possibly how my dad felt when he had to go before his congregation and tell them that God had revealed to him that he was misinterpreting some things in the Bible. People got mad and left the church. To keep from losing people, he could have recanted and said maybe he was wrong. But he didn't because the Bible tells us in James 4:17, "Therefore to him that knoweth to do good, and doeth it not, to him it is a sin." Once he learned the truth, he had to stand with that or be in sin—no matter who walked away because of it. Others around you may not accept it at first, if at all, but you still have to take the truth and walk with it if you want to be free from the curse of disobedience. Sometimes, this means you may have to disassociate from these family members. Matthew 19:29 tells us: "And everyone that hath forsaken houses, or brethren, or sisters, or father, or mother, or wife, or children, or lands, for my name's sake, shall receive a hundredfold, and shall inherit everlasting life." Also, in Matthew 10:14, we read: "And whoever will not receive you nor hear your words, when you depart from that house or city, shake off the dust from your feet." That stands for family members as well. A few verses down in this chapter, verse 22, says, "And you will be hated for my name's sake. But he who endures to the end will be saved." God will send people into your life that will help you grow in him. Don't let foolishness keep you from Christ, ultimately making you lose heaven. As we head to part two of this book, keep searching to free yourself and your family from learned behavior and walk in the freedom of the truth.

Part Two

Chapter Seven

Words Can Hurt More Than Sticks and Stones

Novella lived a miserable life. Everything she ever attempted to achieve blew up in her face. She finished high school and got married just before entering college. Halfway through her junior year, she discovered she was pregnant. She tried hard to keep up with her grades, but no matter how hard she tried, she couldn't. Her problems with her husband, Dan, were terrible, and they got worse every day. One day, just after the baby was born, she found a note saying the marriage was over. Later, she discovered he had been seeing someone else and left his family to be with her. What was she supposed to do? She is almost 23, a college dropout, a single mom, no job, no education to get a decent job, and no family to turn to for help. There was no way she was calling her parents—no way she would hear, "I told you so." Novella recalled her parents' harsh words when she made childhood mistakes. They'd yell at her when she did a chore wrong or received a bad grade in school. Her parents would scream at her, calling her a no-good-for-nothing and saying she would never amount to anything. And every time they beat her, they'd tell her she was unlovable, and that is why they were constantly hitting her.

Before long, Novella found herself in another relationship. Initially, Jim seemed like a dream come true. He was loving towards both her and her baby. Things stayed this way for about two years. Suddenly, Jim was laid off from work. Unable to handle the stress of not being able to provide for his family, he turned to alcohol for comfort. One night, he came home drunk and took his frustration out on Novella, beating her so severely that she could hardly move. This continued for several months until Jim struck Novella's 3-year-old daughter one day. On that day, when he left the house, Novella packed a bag and left

Jim. Once again, she was alone, just as "they" had predicted. What her parents said seemed to be coming true as her life turned into a mess. She felt unwanted and unloved, and it seemed like she was destined to be a failure, just as 'they' had said. On many occasions, she had reached out to her family and friends for advice or support, only to be told that she had caused this to happen because she was so worthless. That may not have been the words they used, but things like "You shouldn't be wasting so much time in college when you should be working." Or "I told you that you would never have a successful marriage." Then there's, "What are you doing that causes these men to act this way toward you." Each time she would reach out to people, it only left her feeling worse until she deemed it useless to reach out and decided she would accept the fate she had been handed.

A few years later, her life took a dramatic turn for the better. Huddled in the corner of a cold concert parking lot, she held her daughter close for warmth under her battered, oversized coat when two strangers approached to ask about their condition. Upon learning that she had a child, the strangers invited her to their soup kitchen for a hot meal and warmth. That night, they had a hot meal and slept in a warm bed for the first time in weeks. Over the next month, Novella was placed in an apartment and had the paperwork to re-enroll in college. She still didn't know why these strangers were so kind to her, but she was so thankful that God had sent her someone who cared enough to help her get back on the right track. Even though they were strangers, they had shown more love than she had ever seen in her lifetime. Trusting people was still an issue for her. How does she know these people won't just desert her like everyone else? What do they want from her? Maybe they will try to take her child from her. That little girl is all she has. But then, what if they have no underlying motives? What if they are genuinely just being nice? For no reason? She was definitely going to have to adjust to this new approach to life.

If you didn't notice from the title and the above short story, this chapter is about the power of your words. Proverbs 18:21 says, "Death and life are in the power of the tongue, and they that love it shall eat the fruit thereof." This proverb notes the often-ignored fact that words are powerful. Verbal attacks, themselves, cannot break bones. Recall the childhood chant—Sticks and stones may break my bones, but words will never hurt me. However, speech can inspire positive and negative responses. It can build up or tear apart. Other Scriptures note the immense power of words, such as Proverbs 10:19, "When words are many, transgression is not lacking, but whoever restrains his lips is prudent." Proverbs 15:1-4 tells us, "A soft answer turns away wrath, but a harsh word stirs anger. The tongue of the wise commends knowledge, but the mouths of fools pour out folly. The eyes of the Lord are in every place, keeping watch on the evil and the good. A gentle tongue is a tree of life, but its perverseness breaks spirit." And we can't forget James 3:5-8, "So also the tongue is a small member, yet it boasts of great things. How great a forest is set ablaze by such a small fire! And the tongue is a fire, a world of unrighteousness. The tongue is set among members, staining the whole body, setting on fire the entire course of life, and set on fire by hell. For every kind of beast and bird, of reptile and sea creature, can be tamed and has been tamed by mankind, but no human being can tame the tongue. It is a restless evil, full of deadly poison." Words can cut deep, so deep that some scars never heal.

When we realize that words are not simply sounds caused by our mouths shaping air passing through our larynx, we understand that words have real power. God spoke the world into being by the power of His words. Humans are made in God's image, and our words also have power. To be clear, human words do not have the power to manifest reality; that's God's power, not ours. However, our words do more than convey information; they impact people. The power of our words can burden one's spirit and even stir up hatred and violence. Words can exacerbate wounds and inflict them directly. Alternatively, words can build up and be life-changing. Ephesians 4:29 says, "Let no corrupt communication proceed out of your mouth, but that which is good to the use of edifying, that it may minister grace unto the hearers." Of all the creatures on this planet, only humans can communicate through the spoken word. The power to use words is a unique and powerful gift from God. Words are so important that we will give an account of what we say when we stand before the Lord Jesus Christ. Jesus said, "But I tell you that men will have to give account on the day of judgment for every careless word they have spoken. For by your words, you will be acquitted, and by your words, you will be condemned" (Matthew 12:36-37).

The apostle Paul wrote, "Do not let any unwholesome talk come out of your mouths, but only what is helpful for building others up according to their needs, that it may benefit those who listen" (Ephesians 4:29). Vulgar humor, dirty jokes, and foul language have no place in the life of a Christian. Instead, our speech is to be characterized by "only what is helpful for building others up according to their needs, that it may benefit those who listen." Colossians 3:16; 4:6 says, "Let the word of Christ dwell in you richly; teach and admonish one another in all wisdom; and with gratitude in your hearts sing psalms, hymns, and spiritual songs to God." 4:6—"Let your conversation always be full of grace, seasoned with salt, so that you may know how to answer everyone." Helpful, edifying, meeting needs, and beneficial—these are our descriptive goals for the words we use. Solomon also notes that speech has consequences for the speaker, "I tell you, on the day of judgment, people will give account for every careless word they speak" (Matthew 12:36).

Let's delve deeper into Proverbs 18:21, which states, "Death and life are in the power of the tongue, and those who love it will eat of its fruit." When the text mentions "those who love 'it'," the "it" refers to the tongue. The "tongue" symbolizes the words spoken because words can either bring death or life. "Those who love 'it'" appreciate the power of language and use their words to achieve their goals. These goals can be positive (i.e., giving life) or negative (i.e., causing death). However, the proverb also emphasizes that the person speaking will experience the consequences of their words. An interesting point is that the effect the words have on the listener is also the effect they have on the speaker. The verse from the book of Proverbs suggests that a person who "lives by their words" will "die by their words." Positive words can bring success and safety, while negative words can bring disaster.

The story of Novella at the beginning of this chapter illustrates the impact of hurtful words commonly used in many homes and families today. I have witnessed it in my own family. It's disheartening to see how some family members are so determined to bring each other down. Novella's upbringing was filled with people who were supposed to love and support her, but instead, they convinced her that she had no future. They convinced her that she was worthless and unlovable. This type of verbal abuse is what is known as a spoken curse. Many people spend much of their adult years believing they are genuinely worthless, just like Novella. They may feel that they are doomed to live a life of gloom and question why God made them this way and let bad things happen to them. Growing up in this environment can make it hard to unlearn these beliefs. It can take years, if ever, to convince someone that they weren't created by God to be treated this way.

Words have immense power, and we need to be mindful of how we use them. Have you heard the phrase "hurt people hurt people"? In Matthew 12:34, it says, "For out of the abundance of the heart the mouth speaketh." What's in your heart will come out through your words and actions. After years of struggling to overcome trauma, I realized the need to build a relationship with Christ to understand my true self. If you've suffered similar abuse, allow Christ to heal you, breaking the cycle of misusing words. If not, the trauma may be passed on. Recognize that you may speak to your children in a harmful way and take steps to stop this cycle. Understanding your identity in Christ is key to stopping it, and that begins with knowing Him.

Letting go of hurt can be difficult. To break free from that pain, you must learn to forgive yourself and others and allow God to heal you from the inside out. In my family, I often witnessed adults expressing negative beliefs about themselves and passing those beliefs on to the children. This is not right. We need to consider how God wants us to treat children and avoid causing harm at a young age. We should stand up for the defenseless, show them love, and teach them about love through Jesus Christ. Let's reflect on this verse: "Open your mouth for the mute, for the rights of all who are destitute. Judge righteously, defend the rights of the poor and needy" (Proverbs 31:8-9). Be careful how you speak in anger. The Bible tells us to be angry and sin not. In anger, you can easily place a curse on someone, putting one on yourself in return. Have you considered the times people have been angry at you? Communicate with God to protect yourself from such curses and use your words wisely... Remember that you will be held accountable for every word on Judgment Day.

Chapter Eight

No Gossip or Backbiting Zone

Now that we have covered one point of word curses let's look at another: Talking badly about people behind their backs. The Bible has several Scriptures on confidentiality, gossip, and openness among the body of Christ. Christians are called upon to share their problems with one another. Galatians 6:2 states, "Bear ye one another's burdens, and so fulfill the law of Christ." In James 5:16, we are instructed to "Confess your faults one to another, and pray one for another, that ye may be healed." However, is it appropriate to discuss someone else's problem with a third party? What should leadership teams do when deciding on a member's course of action? How can a teacher, youth pastor, or other counselor-type

79

position seek help in understanding a difficult situation? Furthermore, what should a friend do if they know something significant about another friend, but the friend is unwilling to share the problem? Lastly, how should you react if a friend says, "I've got something to share, but you have to promise not to tell anyone," Or "By the way, what I told you was in confidence"? The Bible doesn't provide clear-cut instructions for every situation we face under grace. Instead, it outlines fundamental principles, with love being the most important. Loving someone doesn't have a one-size-fits-all approach. Believers are encouraged to follow the guidance of the Holy Ghost and grow in their own discernment. As they become more discerning, they will be better able to determine the most loving approach to take in each situation.

You may be wondering why this subject is essential when discussing curses. Reflecting on what you have read so far, you will see that how you treat people determines your life course. Have you heard the saying "What goes around, comes around"? Galatians 6:7-9 says, "Be not deceived, God is not mocked; for whatever a man sows, that he will also reap." This applies to all areas of life, including how we treat others. Jesus himself tells us to love one another in John 13:34. God doesn't like when we mistreat each other. When someone tells us something confidently, they don't give you information to turn it into the next town gossip. So many people's reputation gets ruined by this one thing right here! If someone comes looking for a friend and you don't have the knowledge to help them, can you go to someone else with their issue? Yes, but names do not have to be mentioned. If names are mentioned, it becomes gossip. You should only give enough information about the issue to gain more knowledge on the subject and only inquire from a trusted person. It should be limited to how many people are included in your quest for answers. On another note, let's say you are a youth group leader, and someone's child discloses to you that they are contemplating suicide; in this case, you should consult with the parents of that child. And get the child the help it needs. This is what is meant above about having discernment. It will lead you to the right thing to do.

Gossipers? We live in a world that loves gossip. Pick up a newspaper, go on social media, or any other public outlet; it doesn't take long to realize that the world thrives on gossiping about things that are none of their business. God cares about the words that come out of our mouths. And how we use our words impacts how we show the love of Christ to the people around us—and how we don't show that love. Our mouths are very often reflective of our hearts. It does not honor the Lord or the people in our lives when we talk behind others' backs or spread rumors about people. The Bible speaks sternly on this subject. Exodus 23:1 says, "Thou shalt not raise a false report. Put not thine hand with the wicked to be an unrighteous witness." Put plainly—"You shall not spread a false report. You shall not join hands with a wicked man to be a malicious witness" (ESV). James 1:26—If any man among you seems to be religious, and bridleth not his tongue, but deceiveth his own heart, this man's religion is vain." And Psalm 34:13 says, "Keep your tongue from evil and your lips from speaking deceit." Then lastly— Ephesians 4:29 says, "Let no corrupting talk come out of your mouth, but only such as is good for building up, as fits the occasion that it may give grace to those who hear." It's clear to see that our mouths get us into a lot of trouble. We profess to believe one thing, but then we are often betrayed by what comes out of our mouths. Remember that Jesus said that out of the abundance of the heart the mouth speaks. When we set out to spread gossip or lies about people, we are showing the world who WE really are. It doesn't matter what you profess or call yourself—your speech betrays you.

Remember when Jesus had been captured, and Peter stood without and denied he knew him? Matthew 26:73 says, "And after a while came unto him, they that stood by, and said to Peter, Surely, thou art one of them; for thy speech bewrayeth thee. Then he began to curse and swear, saying, I know not the man. And immediately, the cock crew" Peter didn't seem to realize what a compliment he had received that day. "I know you are one of Jesus' followers because you act and talk just like him." Wow! That is what we should all be striving for in life. You may say you have lived that way, but people have tainted your name with lies. Jesus has a word for you on that, too; Psalm 43, if read in the King James Version, says, "Judge me, O God, and plead my cause against an ungodly nation: O deliver me from the deceitful and unjust man." What the psalmist is saying here is, "Search my heart and find that I have been true and vindicate me." So, don't fret when people try to smudge your name—that's their punishment, not yours, as long as you are quiet and let him deal with it. 1 Thessalonians 4:11 says, "And that you study to be quiet, and to do your own business, and to work with your own hands, as we commanded you;"

We can learn a lot when we discipline ourselves to listen more than we talk. Big talkers are hard to teach. They think they already know everything they need to know, and they constantly express their opinions. Wise people have learned that more wisdom can be gained by listening, observing, and not rushing to judgment. Proverbs 10:19 says, "When words are many, transgression is not lacking, but whoever restrains his lips is prudent." The old adage is correct: "It is better to remain silent and be thought a fool than to open one's mouth and remove all doubt." How many relationships have been damaged or ruined because we were slow to listen and quick to speak? How many mistakes could have been avoided had we only listened instead of talking? Remember James 1:19? "Wherefore, my beloved brethren, let every man be swift to hear, slow to speak, slow to wrath." We are being instructed here to trust God, even during hard times. In fact, believers are to consider their hardships as "joy" since trials are how God strengthens our faith. Those who trust and obey God learn to adjust the speed of their listening and speaking. If God is truly in control, we can afford to take the time to understand. Rather than shooting from the hip, we can respond helpfully. Doubting that God is in control speeds up our mouths and slows our minds.

We have all seen the wreckage that gossip can cause: feelings hurt, trust destroyed, relationships ruined— above all, an atmosphere of mistrust and fear. People feel reluctant to open up out of fear people will broadcast it. Also, people may not open up about serious problems or may sanitize their versions of those problems unless we can offer them the safety of confidentiality. Proverbs speak a lot on this subject; chapter 11, verses 12 and 13, is one of those places; it says, "Whoever belittles his neighbor lacks sense, but a man of understanding remains silent. Whoever goes about slandering reveals secrets, but he who is trustworthy in spirit keeps a thing covered." Then, in Chapter 19, verse 9, we have, "Whoever covers an offense seeks love, but he who repeats a matter separates close friends." Finally, in Proverbs 20:19, "Whoever goes about slandering reveals secrets; therefore, do not associate with a simple babbler." Merely avoiding gossip isn't all we have to consider in this passage. Being a true child of God means that we also practice confidentiality. The Cambridge online dictionary defines confidentiality as "The fact of private information being kept secret." It's that simple. So why do so many people struggle with practicing this? Maybe because they haven't learned to bridle their tongue?

Not only is it inappropriate to share other people's private information with others, but what's even worse is that the information often gets distorted or misrepresented, making it untrue. The Bible emphasizes the severity of lying in Revelations 21:8, stating that liars will face consequences. As Christians, we are called to support and uplift one another, not to use sensitive information for gossip. 1 Thessalonians 5:11-13 encourages us to encourage and build each other up and to respect and honor those who guide and teach us. When someone confides in you, it's best to keep it confidential and only share it with others if necessary. If you're concerned, seeking advice is acceptable, but respecting the confidant's privacy is important. Before sharing someone's business with others, it's good practice to ask yourself a few questions...

- Is the person you are consulting capable of offering valuable advice?
- Is the driving force behind action fueled by concern or curiosity?

- Are you reaching out for support, or are you divulging someone's sensational secrets in order to elicit a reaction from others?

- Are we genuinely seeking input, or are we simply venting frustration?

The Bible sternly prohibits gossip but encourages confiding in others to uplift each other in Christ. Keep in mind that your treatment of others can determine whether your life is filled with blessings or curses. When someone confides in you, it's crucial to handle their trust responsibly. Demonstrating trustworthiness by keeping confidential information, especially personal or sensitive details shared by others, is key. Do you engage in gossip? Are you the one who shares stories to outdo others in public? Or maybe people come to you with shocking tales of others' sins or embarrassments? On the other hand, are you someone who hoards secrets, reluctant to confide even when unsure how to proceed? Building a strong prayer life and cultivating godly discernment can provide guidance in navigating these complex situations.

Gossiping, talebearing, backbiting, telling lies—whatever you want to call it—has detrimental effects. The Bible condemns gossip as untrustworthy and meddlesome (Proverbs 11:13; 20:19; 26:20; 1 Timothy 5:13) and even as worthy of death (Romans 1:29, 32). While the Scriptures do not provide a specific definition of gossip in one location, they describe gossip in action and tie it to the character of people participating in this sin. The sin of gossip can be summarized as bearing bad news behind someone's back out of an immoral heart. "If it's true, then it's not gossip" is a common misconception, but needlessly sharing shameful truths about someone else is gossip. One biblical phrase for this kind of speech is "a bad report," such as what Joseph brought against his brothers (Genesis 37:2). Just because someone did something wrong does not mean we need to talk about it with others. We might spread a wicked story of what might soon happen to someone. For example, when King David was sick, his enemies acted concerned when they visited him, then secretly celebrated his projected downfall and spread the story that he was about to die (Psalm 41:5-8). That was also gossip. So, we need to be careful when any conversation begins to steer toward the topic of other people and ask ourselves, "Is this story true? How do I know?" or "Is this story mine to tell? Is it his to tell me?"

It's crucial to keep in mind that the act of gossiping only occurs when the individual who is the subject of the conversation is not present. For instance, I have drawn examples from the Bible to illustrate this point, but I'm confident that you have your own experiences with this as well. It's true for all of us. While we may not always have control over what others say to us, we do have the power to control our own responses. Additionally, we have the ability to decide what we contribute to a conversation. It's important to make a habit of refraining from discussing others' private matters unless what we have to say is genuinely praiseworthy or uplifting. Do you recognize the pattern in the book? The most detrimental curse on our bloodline is our treatment of each other. I will emphasize this point repeatedly until its significance is fully understood. We can't go on mistreating each other if we want to be free from the curse of sins. That's that—it's that clear; it really is that simple: change how you treat people. Dispose of all corrupt and evil learned behavior. Or die under the curse.

Conferral	Gossip
Fueled by a strong desire to help people and strengthen the community of those who believe in Christ.	Lack of concern for others and a desire to inflict harm while boosting one's own status.
Consults only with	Feel free to engage in

responsible individuals who can provide assistance.	conversations with anyone they like, regardless of the impact it may have on them.
Confers only on current issues.	Talks about past, dead, purely personal issues.
Done in addition to talking to the person if needed.	Done instead of talking to the person if required.
Understands that it's absolutely essential to vividly convey the context of the problem to the individual you are conferring with.	Neglects or distorts the crucial context of the problem.
Inspires greater trust, fosters open and honest communication, and minimizes gossip about individuals or situations.	Fosters a culture of fear around openness and exacerbates gossip about the individual or situation.
Discouraging the sharing of irrelevant or interfering information, as it detracts from our ability to show love and compassion for others.	"Compelling others to disclose information for the sheer pleasure of being 'in the know.'"
Respect the boundaries of "need-to-know" information and uphold the value of discretion.	"Demands to be in the know about everything."

I want to share a powerful example that fits this chapter with you. In 2003, I found myself in a highly abusive relationship. Tragically, this relationship culminated in a violent incident where I was shot, and my partner was subsequently incarcerated. Following this traumatic event, I made the difficult decision to leave my hometown and did not return until ten years later, in 2013. Whenever I traveled to visit my dad, I found myself chuckling at the preposterous things that some of my family members would say. It was a rare occurrence for me to return home, happening just once or twice a year, and the primary reason for this was to spend time with my dad. During these visits, I didn't communicate with anyone else, nor did I meet up with anyone else, and there were no calls to check in on me. Despite this, I was surprised to discover that certain individuals with too much free time would fabricate imaginative tales about what was supposedly happening in my life. My own family did everything they could in their power to destroy my image and reputation.

I have always cherished my privacy and enjoy spending quiet evenings at home. I find solace in reading books, writing, and watching TV. Occasionally, I love to escape to the mountains for a peaceful walk. While I did go dancing on rare occasions, I've never been inclined toward wild or extravagant parties. After becoming a parent, I had even less time for personal pursuits. My focus shifted entirely to caring for my children. It was during these years that I would sit and share laughter with my dad while he spent time with his grandchildren. However, I'm not the only one who got done this way. If they were talking 'to' me, well, they chose a different name. I only want you to remember that talking about people is never okay. Not unless you are genuinely concerned about them. The information you receive should not be used to degrade others, as doing so ultimately only does harm to yourself. What goes around does come back around. Be careful how you treat people.

Chapter Nine

What are you telling yourself?

Did you know that the words you choose to speak can have a profound impact on the course of your life? Every day, how you speak to yourself and the words you use to describe your life, career, future, and home have an incredible power to shape your reality. It's essential to understand that you possess divine authority over your own life, and as such, your words hold significant influence. When you consistently use words filled with hope, faith, and positivity, you actively pave the way for blessings and favorable outcomes. On the other hand, if you tend to speak words that are tinged with fear and negativity, you might inadvertently set in motion a series of unfavorable events and outcomes, such as curses. The book of Proverbs reminds us of the power of our words, stating that "death and life are in the power of the tongue, and those who love it will eat its fruits." Similarly, Jesus cautioned us about the impact of our words, saying, "For by thy words thou shalt be justified, and by thy words, thou shalt be condemned" (Matthew 12:37). It's important to be mindful of self-imposed curses, which are negative confessions and responses that can have a detrimental effect on our lives. For instance, imagine if I were to ask you, 'How's life?' and you say...

- "Wow, this is really tough."
- "Things are really tough right now."
- "I've exhausted every possible option, but it seems there's no way through"
- "I'm dying."
- "There is no hope."
- "These kids are killing me."
- "This job is truly draining the life out of me."
- "I feel like I'm just wasting away here."
- "My husband is always such a pain."
- "My wife is being difficult. She is driving me crazy."

- "This economy is absolutely crippling"
- "I just keep feeling more and more frustrated."
- "I will be dead soon!"
- "This child is hopeless."

When you use words like these, it might seem like you're simply describing the current circumstances. However, they are actually powerful negative affirmations that can shape future realities. The Bible says: "He that keepeth his mouth keepeth his life: but he that openeth wide his lips shall have destruction" (Proverbs 13:3). "Pleasant words are as a honeycomb, sweet to the soul, and health to the bones" (Proverbs 16:24). "Whoso keepeth his mouth and his tongue keepeth his soul from troubles" (Proverbs 21:23). "But those things which proceed out of the mouth come forth from the heart; they defile the man" (Matthew 15:18). "Let no corrupt communication proceed out of your mouth, but that which is good to the use of edifying, that it may minister grace unto the hearers" (Ephesians 4:29). The scriptures emphasize the seriousness of the warnings regarding our words. They highlight the impact our words can have on our lives, either bringing about success or causing harm. While it's important to learn how to revoke curses, it's equally crucial to embrace

God's correction and guidance in order to completely steer clear of these harmful effects.

I remember a friend from several years ago who possessed an unwavering dedication to prayer. I always admired her profound commitment to prayer. She had a habit of waking up in the depths of the night and delving into extensive, fervent prayer sessions that lasted for hours. Whenever I initiated my own prayer routine, she was already deeply engrossed in hers, and even after I concluded, she would persist in her devout prayer. Her unparalleled devotion to prayer was truly remarkable. Unfortunately, whenever I engage her in conversations about life, her responses are overwhelmingly negative. Her speech is saturated with disappointment, fear, and a relentless focus on failure, leaving me to ponder how she can spend endless hours in prayer while seemingly unable to recognize any positivity in life. Attempting to offer my encouragement is invariably met with dismissal. It's a perplexing paradox that consistently eludes my comprehension. Her journey was marked by a multitude of daunting challenges that preceded her profound realization of the divine calling upon her life. Sadly, the weight of these setbacks had molded her perspective, causing her to harbor modest expectations despite her unwavering commitment to prayer. This mindset was openly conveyed in her conversations. Intriguingly, when our paths crossed a few years back, it was evident that her experiences had not significantly transitioned from the narrative she had painted years earlier.

Life is a journey full of twists and turns, presenting us with countless challenges and setbacks. It's often a tough and demanding road for all of us to navigate. However, it's essential to maintain a positive outlook despite the difficulties. We must resist the urge to let our problems dictate our thoughts and expectations for the future. Allowing our challenges to shape our mindset can lead to the imposition of self-limiting beliefs, thereby erecting invisible barriers that may leave us questioning the origin of our struggles. We must strive to safeguard ourselves from experiencing the same hardships that my friend and many others have endured. Take the time to pray and seek guidance from God to transform your perspective on life. Request His insight into the underlying causes of your desires and feelings of defeat and ask Him to reveal your identity and purpose in Him. He always responds to sincere heartfelt pleas. Embrace His presence and allow Him to bring about a profound transformation in your heart and life.

Changing how you see you

Before I end this chapter, I believe it's crucial to reiterate the significance of our words when discussing others. The Bible emphasizes the power of our words, highlighting their potential to bring either life or death. When we speak negatively of others, we not only impact them but also invite negative consequences into our own lives. This is a powerful reminder to be mindful of our speech, as it can shape our reality. The age-old advice, 'If you can't say something nice, don't say anything at all,' serves as a valuable daily reminder. I prefer to express this as, 'Be mindful of your words, as they have the potential to return to bite you.' When faced with any perceived curse affecting you or your family, I would reflect upon how you interact with others first. Remember this message: 'Adopting the habit of refraining from speaking ill of yourself or others would be the best practice to follow. Furthermore, a friend once shared with me her guiding principle: 'If it's not about me, then it's none of my business,' and she consistently questions, 'Is this something I would want to be said about me?'

However, when we make a habit of constantly degrading ourselves, then we see no problem in doing the same thing to others. "Your nose looks terrible in that picture. Your legs look gross. You are not a good mom. You are lazy for not working out!" Are these lines from that movie about the bullies, 'Mean Girls'? Nope. These statements were said by me—to me. If those exact words had been spoken by someone else, it would have undoubtedly resulted in significant emotional distress and could have potentially led to some form of vindictive action. At times, I grapple with the challenge of managing negative self-talk, feeling as though I am giving the critical voice within me an unwarranted spotlight. This experience can be quite overwhelming if I fail to address it, underscoring the importance of learning to navigate and control this internal struggle.

When my daughter brought home a new puppy, I was instantly taken with her adorable little face. However, I soon realized that despite her cuteness, she could be a bit of a handful. The little furball had a tendency to be a bit feisty at times, and her boundless energy turned her into a whirlwind of chaos. Despite this, I constantly remind myself that she is just a puppy and needs time and practice to learn how to behave. Similarly, we larger, less furry creatures need practice to learn new skills, too! A common misconception among Christians is that we can quickly eliminate negative behaviors, give them to God, and move on effortlessly. Unfortunately, giving something to God doesn't mean it magically disappears. Learning from God requires dedication, patience, and yes, practice. We must actively work on our behaviors, seeking guidance and strength from our faith to make lasting changes. Just as it takes time and effort for us to develop new skills, it also takes time and effort to transform our thoughts and actions in alignment with our spiritual beliefs.

I frequently find myself in situations where I'm imparting advice to my children, and it feels like I'm repeating the same old clichés, like a broken record. I often emphasize the importance of hard work and practice, emphasizing that it may be challenging, but the effort is worthwhile because it instills better discipline. At times, I can't help but feel a bit exasperated with my own words, even though I know deep down that they hold true. Before we embark on the skill-training journey of learning how to stop negative self-talk, let's take a moment to thoroughly explore the reasons and motivations behind it. Understanding the significance of the 'why' is crucial for maintaining focus and determination throughout the training process.

Negative self-talk can be harmful because it can lead to increased stress, anxiety, and decreased self-esteem. When we constantly tell ourselves we're not good enough or that we should be doing more, it can have a significant impact on our mental health. Specifically in terms of health, negative self-talk can create pressure to adhere to strict dietary and exercise regimens, which can lead to unhealthy behaviors and attitudes towards food and fitness. For instance, we might feel compelled to eat more vegetables, walk more, lift weights, do cardio, and stretch frequently, which can become overwhelming and unsustainable. When you incorporate spiritual disciplines, such as prayer and meditating on the Word of God, along with the expectations of maintaining relationships, fulfilling job duties, and managing routine chores, life can feel like an endless stream of responsibilities clamoring for your attention. Have you ever longed for the opportunity to sit down and have a heart-to-heart conversation with Jesus, asking Him, "What is the single most important thing that you want me to focus on?" It's an intriguing thought, isn't it? Interestingly, someone has already had that conversation with Him. Someone already got that answer for us. In Matthew 22:36, a man who seemed confident in his understanding of the commandments tested Jesus by posing the question, "Teacher, which is the greatest commandment in the Law?" This inquiry aimed to challenge Jesus's knowledge and understanding of the religious laws and commandments. Here's the moment we've all been waiting for...in verse 37, Jesus responded to the question by saying, "Love the Lord your God with all your heart and with all your soul and with all your mind. This is the first and greatest commandment. And the second is like it: Love your neighbor as yourself. On these two commandments depend all the Law and the Prophets." Wow! This is a powerful statement, as it condenses the numerous commandments from the Old Testament into two fundamental expectations: Love for God and love for others.

I wonder if the religious scholar went back to his home, sat down in a quiet corner, and spent hours delving deep into contemplation and introspection. I genuinely hope so! It's all too easy to casually breeze through that familiar passage, but if we genuinely immerse ourselves in its wisdom and apply its principles, it has the power to revolutionize our entire outlook and approach to life. All the expectations we place on ourselves can be filtered through those two commands. For example: "Is (fill in the blank) helping me love God and others well? A question to start with is, "Does the presence of negative self-talk impede our ability to fulfill the mission of loving God and others?" When we take the enemy's perspective into account, it is clear that indulging in negative self-talk can significantly divert our focus from our intended goals. Attacking the home base exemplifies a potent way in which this diversion can unfold. When I am feeling low about my physical appearance or areas where I perceive myself to be lacking, my attention is predominantly directed inward, and I find myself dwelling less on thoughts of God. In these moments, I might even experience feelings of resentment towards God.

Have you ever driven a car that turned out to be a real piece of junk? Who's to blame for the car's issues? Well, it's possible that the driver plays a part in the car's problems, but most of the blame would usually fall on the car's creator, right? Similarly, maintaining a constant negative view of oneself implies a belief that the creator made an error in the design. This negative self-perception may arise from a persistent sense of discontent and the misbelief that one's creation is flawed. What a triumph for the enemy if we succumb to self-doubt and question God!

Additionally, let's not disregard the fact that speaking ill of ourselves can swiftly breed feelings of envy and bitterness toward others! The principle of 'loving others like myself' is fundamentally flawed if I am unable to love myself. It is essential to recognize that in order to genuinely extend love and compassion to others, I must first cultivate a deep sense of self-love and acceptance. Only then can I authentically and wholeheartedly embody the concept of 'loving others like myself.' Enough dwelling on the problem! The adversary, Satan, has already been defeated, and we are victorious. Let's delve into how God empowers us to triumph in this battle.

We were made for good works (Ephesians 2:10). It's time to eliminate distractions and wholeheartedly focus on fulfilling that purpose! To conquer negative self-talk, we must uproot the negativity and expose the falsehoods. Although I've never had much success with gardening, I've always been drawn to gardening analogies. I believe it's crucial to take a closer look at the metaphorical "soil" of our hearts, especially when we're grappling with specific challenges, such as negative self-talk. Just as tending to the soil is essential for healthy plant growth, nurturing our inner selves is vital for our emotional well-being. Is the soil of our hearts overrun with weeds that hinder the love and truth of God from taking root? Negative thoughts about ourselves often originate from false beliefs deeply embedded in our hearts. This can be linked to generational curses, where negative patterns and beliefs are passed down through generations. As Christians, we have a powerful weapon in the form of our faith and the truth of God's word, which is even more potent in dispelling these lies than Roundup is at eliminating weeds. 2 Corinthians 10:5 says, "We demolish arguments and every pretension that sets itself up against the knowledge of God, and we take captive every thought to make it obedient to Christ."

When confronted with lies and deceptive beliefs, they will not stand a chance when examined in the presence of the Son of the most high God. How can we practically bring these falsehoods to trial and expose them for what they are? Can we delve into the depths of our minds, extract our thoughts, and confine them within a cage? As much as we wish for such control, it eludes us. Nevertheless, God has equipped us with powerful tools, such as His word, the practice of journaling, the act of praying, and the support of fellow believers to aid us in uncovering and dispelling falsehoods within our hearts. We have a responsibility to tend to the soil, ensuring that it receives the care and sustenance it needs. Once the soil is cleared of weeds, it is essential to provide young plants with the necessary care and nourishment to support their growth. Similarly, as we strive to grow spiritually with the Lord, we, too, require nurturing and sustenance to thrive. One fundamental aspect of self-care that we consistently require is emotional nourishment. Negative self-talk often serves as a shield for deeper emotions. For instance, when I berate myself for being lazy and failing to exercise sufficiently, it's often a result of feeling guilty, weak, and ashamed due to the childhood taunting I experienced about my weight. It's essential to recognize and address these underlying feelings in order to cultivate a sense of emotional well-being. Although these feelings aren't based on facts, it's essential to acknowledge and address them. Unresolved pain can linger, but seeking care allows for progress and healing. The ultimate healer, Jesus Christ, is always ready and willing to help us in our time of need. In 1 Peter 5:6-8, we are encouraged to cast all our worries and concerns upon Him because He genuinely cares for us. When we lay our burdens at the feet of Christ, it creates a space for us to receive and accept God's truth about our immense worth and value in His eyes.

Let's carefully remove the unnecessary branches and trim away anything that hinders growth. I hope you are feeling prepared to confront and overcome negative self-talk. However, before you charge ahead to conquer your challenges, let's take the time to delve into some additional information that is crucial to know. This may not be the most enjoyable aspect of learning to prune, but it is essential for your personal growth and development. In the book of John, chapter 15, there is a powerful metaphor about pruning unnecessary branches to yield a more abundant harvest (see John 15:2). This metaphor underscores the idea that removing what is unproductive or unnecessary in our lives can lead to greater blessings and growth. While pruning may initially seem harsh, it's essential to understand that this spiritual process, when administered by the Lord with grace and love, is designed to foster our personal and spiritual development rather than inflict punishment. It serves as a reminder that sometimes we need to let go of certain things in order to make room for new growth and abundance in our lives. The next time you find yourself being critical or nit-picky in your thoughts, try taking a moment to bring those thoughts before God and evaluate them from a spiritual perspective. Consider whether these thoughts align with God's plans for you and if there could be something that God is guiding you to let go of.

In this chapter, it is emphasized that when we receive Christ's unconditional love and forgiveness, it fundamentally transforms our ability to love God and others. The text highlights the idea that trying to love God and others from a place of emptiness, inadequacy, hatred, or guilt is a challenging and often unsustainable endeavor. Instead, the focus is on the transformative power of Christ's love, which allows our hearts to overflow with love rooted in genuine relationship and passion, rather than being driven by a sense of obligation. Furthermore, the chapter delves into the concept of developing a deep and personal relationship with Christ, which enables us to truly comprehend and internalize His love for us. This understanding, in turn, leads to a profound sense of self-love and acceptance, as we learn to see ourselves through Christ's eyes. Consequently, this newfound self-love enables us to authentically love others, recognizing and embracing the universal truth that we are all flawed and in need of the perfect love that is found in Christ.

Don't allow the labels and judgments of others to shape your self-worth. Your true value comes from your identity in Christ. According to His perspective, you are so precious that He sacrificed Himself for you.

Chapter Ten

Demonic Curses

This chapter will delve into the intriguing realms of witchcraft, divination, soothsaying, sorcery, and other forms of demonic curses. The Bible offers profound insights into witchcraft and its related practices. Witchcraft, along with its counterparts such as fortune-telling and necromancy, are deemed as deceptive imitations of genuine spiritual practices by Satan. The Bible explicitly denounces all forms of witchcraft. Throughout history, individuals have encountered supernatural phenomena that God did not approve. The surrounding nations of the Promised Land were steeped in such forbidden practices, and God warned His people sternly against any involvement with them. Deuteronomy 18:9-12 says, "When you enter the land your God is giving you, do not learn to imitate the detestable ways of the nations there. Let no one be found among you who sacrifices their son or daughter in the fire, who practices divination or sorcery, interprets omens, engages in witchcraft, or casts spells, or who is a medium or spiritist or who consults the dead. Anyone who does these things is detestable to the Lord."

Witchcraft is a matter of utmost seriousness in the Bible. According to the Mosaic Law, the punishment for engaging in witchcraft was death (Exodus 22:18, Leviticus 20:27). Notably, 1 Chronicles 10:13 recounts that "Saul died because he was unfaithful to the Lord; he did not keep the word of the Lord and even consulted a medium for guidance." In the New Testament, "sorcery" is derived from the Greek word *"pharmakeia,"* which is the root of the word "pharmacy" (Galatians 5:20; Revelation 18:23). Witchcraft and spiritism frequently involve the ceremonial use of magic potions and manipulative substances. The use of illicit drugs can render individuals vulnerable to demonic intrusion. It is important to note that partaking in activities or consuming substances to achieve an altered state of consciousness is considered a form of witchcraft. It is also important to note that prescription drugs that alter your mind, alcohol, and street drugs are all gateways for demons to enter.

There are only two sources of spiritual power: God and Satan. As stated in Job 1:12, 2 Corinthians 4:4, and Revelation 20:2, Satan's power is only as extensive as God permits, yet it remains formidable. It is crucial to understand that pursuing spirituality, knowledge, or power separate from God is tantamount to idolatry and is closely associated with witchcraft. 1 Samual 15:23 says, "For rebellion is as the sin of witchcraft, and stubbornness is as iniquity and idolatry." The practice of witchcraft is associated with Satan, as he mimics the works of God. For example, when Moses performed miracles before Pharaoh, the magicians were able to replicate these miracles using demonic power (Exodus 8:7). Witchcraft is driven by the desire to predict the future and manipulate events that are beyond our control. These abilities belong only to the Lord. This desire originates from Satan's initial temptation of Eve. "You can be like God" (Genesis 3:5). Since the time of the Garden of Eden, Satan has consistently sought to draw human hearts away from the true worship of God

(Genesis 3:1). He lures people with the allure of power, self-fulfillment, and spiritual enlightenment while bypassing submission to the Lord God. Engaging in witchcraft involves entering into the realm of Satan, and it encompasses more than just traditional practices. Modern entanglements with witchcraft may include activities such as consulting horoscopes, using Ouija boards, participating in Eastern meditation rituals, séance rituals, and ghost hunting (you are demon hunting, only one good ghost, and that is the Holy Ghost; others are demonic). and engaging in particular video and role-playing games. It's essential to recognize that any practice that taps into a power source other than the authority of the Lord Jesus Christ is considered to be a form of witchcraft. Revelation 22:15 includes witches in a list of those who will not inherit eternal life: "Outside are the dogs, those who practice magic arts, the sexually immoral, the murderers, the idolaters, and everyone who loves and practices falsehood."

We don't need to fear Satan's power, but we should stay away from it. 1 John 4:4 says, Greater is he who is in you than he that is in the world." Satan can create much havoc, harm, and destruction, even in the lives of believers (1 Thessalonians 2:18; Job 1:12-18; 1 Corinthians 5:5).

However, if we belong to the Lord Jesus Christ, no power can ultimately defeat us. Isaiah 54:7, "No weapon that is fashioned against you shall succeed and shall refute every tongue that rises against you in judgment. This is the heritage of the servants of the Lord, and their vindication from me declares the Lord." We are overcomers as we "put on the whole armor of God so that you can stand against the devil's schemes" (Ephesians 6:11). When we give our lives to Christ, we must repent. This repentance should include renouncing any involvement with witchcraft, following the example of the early believers in Acts 19:19. Isaiah 8:19 says, "When someone tells you to consult mediums and spirits, who whisper and mutter, should not a people inquire of their God? Why consult the dead on behalf of the living?" When we follow those words to their logical conclusion, we could also ask, "Why seek any power apart from the source of all real power? Why seek spirits who are not the Holy Spirit?" witchcraft and its many counterparts promise spirituality but lead only to emptiness and death (Micah 5:12; Galatians 5:19-21). Only Jesus has the words of life, John 6:68, "Simon Peter answered him, "Lord whom shall we go? You have the words of eternal life".

Satan is roaming the earth looking for a door of opportunity to enter and destroy every life he can. He will paint a picture of innocence that makes it look like what you are experimenting with is just fun and games. The occult is nothing to play with. It seems harmless, but it opens the door to a bigger problem. Did you know that taking your baby to a witch doctor introduces demons into that child's life? Astrology, horoscopes, palm reading, black arts, fortune telling...see what I mean by they can appear harmless? Black magic, white magic, tarot cards, crystal balls, tea leaves, and much more like this. Also, dabbling in false religions opens the door for demonic curses. Buddhism, Hinduism, or any other religion that rejects Jesus as the Christ. Objects in your home such as books on magic (even children's books), charms (i.e., rabbit's foot), anything to ward off evil (i.e., horseshoe, garlic, sage). When you don't realize that the blood of Jesus Christ is more than enough to cover and protect you, you resort to these things...it opens the door for demons to come into your home and life.

Now, look at Isaiah 54:15,17: "Behold, they shall surely gather together, but not by me: whosoever shall gather together against thee shall fall for thy sake. Behold, I have created the smith that bloweth the coals in the fire, and that bringeth forth an instrument for his work; and I have created the waster to destroy. No weapon formed against thee shall prosper, and thou shalt condemn every tongue that shall rise against thee in judgment. This is the heritage of the servants of the Lord, and their righteousness is of me, saith the Lord." The Bible discusses the gathering of evil people who may attempt to inflict harm through witchcraft, curses, and other wicked activities. It acknowledges the prevalence of such wickedness on earth. However, it also provides assurance of victory when these situations are brought before Christ, and His justice is sought through prayer. Mark 7:21 tells us: "For from within, out of the hearts of men, proceed evil thoughts, adulteries, fornications, murders." Then go to Jeremiah 17:9, "The heart is deceitful above all things and desperately wicked: who can know it?" There are people whose minds are so twisted by the devil that they hate the well-being of others. These ruthless individuals will stop at nothing to inflict spiritual anguish, emotional setbacks, and physical ailments on their target. Beware of those who seek to inflict harm through witchcraft, voodoo, sorcery, occultism, or other dark arts. These individuals are relentless in their pursuit to cause damage to their targets. Stay vigilant against their malevolent intentions. Problems created by these types of people are classified as curses from wicked men.

In Numbers 22:6 we read: "Come now therefore, I pray thee, curse for me this people; for they are too mighty for me. Perhaps I shall prevail, that we may smite them, and that I may drive them out of the land; for I know that he whom thou blessest is blessed, and he whom thou cursest is cursed." Here we witness the tale of Balak, the king of Moab, who is determined to obstruct the Israelites from traversing through his land en route to their Promised Land. Doubting the capability of his mighty military to overcome the Israelites, whom he believes are divinely protected, Balak turns to spiritual intervention. In a bid to vanquish the Israelites, he persuades the esteemed prophet and diviner, Balaam, to lay a curse upon them. This gripping account delves into the high-stakes spiritual battle between Balak and the people of Israel. When individuals send curses, arrows, attacks, and evil intentions toward others, they attempt to create spiritual weight and barriers in their victims' lives. These malicious actions inflict significant suffering, hinder their ability to achieve breakthroughs and block the manifestation of God's blessings in their lives. The Bible consistently affirms the profound and intricate realities that shape our everyday lives, offering timeless wisdom and guidance in a world full of uncertainty. Recall Isaiah 54:15 above: "Behold, they shall surely gather together, but not by me: whosoever shall gather together against thee shall fall for thy sake." The Bible warns they will gather, but their victory depends on your permission. Stand firm and do not let them prevail.

When it comes to casting out demons, the Bible tells the best advice on this in the following story. I've revised it into story form. However, you can find it in the Bible in Matthew chapter 17. Starting in verse 14, we see Jesus and three of his disciples returning from the mountain to find a crowd gathered. A desperate father pleads on behalf of his demon-afflicted son, who has seizures and often falls into the water or fire. He tells Jesus that he asked of the disciples, but they could not perform this quest. Jesus, exasperated by the doubt of his disciples, rebukes the demon and heals the boy. When they ask, Jesus tells the disciples their faith was too small to cast out the demon. Even faith as small as a mustard seed is enough to move a mountain. Then, in verse 21, Jesus tells them, However, this kind goeth not out but by prayer and fasting. Spend time in prayer with him, deny yourself the pleasures of food for a time, and spend that time with Christ. In doing so, you are bottling up power to defeat the demonic forces around you. Get rid of all demonic practices and stop dappling into any form of Satanism—including watching it on TV or online. Find a prayer partner and get better results. Matthew 18:19-29 says, "Again I say to you that if two of you agree on earth concerning anything that they ask, it will be done for them by my father in heaven. For where two or three are gathered together in my name, I am there in the midst of them."

Below is a list of items that you want to get rid of from your home	
Occult Books	Covenanted Rings
Satanic Movies	Religious Statues
Sage Burning	Dream Catchers
Ouija Boards	Crystals
Tarot Cards	Evil Books
Evil Toys	Evil Jewelry
Soul Tie Objects	Grave Images
Accursed Figurines	Anything Ungodly

***Descriptions on page

Chapter Eleven

Why is it important to know about curses?

We have covered a lot of information in the previous chapters. This chapter will tie it together and give in-depth information on each subject. I also want to take this time to remind you that I am not writing this book to shame anyone. As a matter of fact, I didn't even want to write this book. As you grow in Christ, you will come to understand that sometimes, he uses our calling for things that we may not feel comfortable doing. I am not a confrontational person. This is a highly contentious subject, and I had reservations about obeying the call. Neglecting spiritual signals, God's leading and divine direction produces the effects of curses. Had I not obeyed, I would have suffered the consequences of disobedience. 1 Samuel 15:22-24 says, "And Samuel said, hath the Lord as great delight in burnt offerings and sacrifices, as in obeying the voice of the Lord? Behold, to obey is better than sacrifice, and to hearken than the fat of rams. For rebellion is as the sin of witchcraft, and stubbornness is as iniquity and idolatry. Because thou hast rejected the word of the Lord, he hath also rejected thee from being king." Read the following verse 24 closely, "And Saul said unto Samuel, I have sinned: because I feared the people and obeyed their voice."

When we fail to acknowledge and heed God's guidance in our hearts, it can hinder the flow of blessings in our lives. Despite devoting extensive time to prayer and fasting, we may not witness corresponding outcomes. Additionally, we might contribute considerable funds and resources to assist the less fortunate and support the church. However, we could still encounter unanswered prayers due to our lack of alignment with God's purpose for our lives. As children of God, it is of utmost importance for us to develop the ability to discern when and how God is communicating with us in our hearts and to follow His guidance willingly. Through obedience, we access God's blessings and find ourselves under His protective care.

I believe that spiritual disobedience attracts the biggest of all curses in life. We invite this curse when we willfully disobey the inner witness of the voice of God. In Job 36:10-12, we read: "He opened their ear to discipline and commanded them to return from iniquity. If they obey and serve him, they shall spend their days in prosperity and their years in pleasure. But if they obey not, they shall perish by the sword, and they shall die without knowledge." It is crucial to consider the scripture's message. Within the Bible, it is stated that if we disregard God's leadership and instruction in our hearts, we will face the risk of perishing by the sword and dying without knowledge. This does not necessarily refer to eternal damnation but rather to the potential exposure to suffering and evil situations that may lead to our demise. At times, we possess an innate sense of what the correct course of action is in a given situation, but we tend to disregard it and carry on. Our spirits may signal to us, conveying a distinct feeling that "this is wrong, and this is the way forward." However, we often seek additional visible signs and confirmations instead of heeding this internal guidance. There is a tendency to anticipate grandiose displays such as thunderous voices, significant dreams, or earth-shaking occurrences. It's essential to recognize that God does not always manifest in such overt and dramatic ways.

Disobeying the teachings of God's word can lead us to commit other sins. In earlier chapters, we explored how our treatment of others can impact our prayers and result in negative consequences in our lives. Being obedient to God's word would lead us to treat others with kindness and respect, in accordance with the guidance provided in the Bible. If we fail to show love and kindness to others, we are not following Christ's teachings as he has instructed us to do. When we wholeheartedly embrace and adhere to the teachings of God's word, we fortify ourselves against being ensnared by detrimental thought patterns and behaviors within our families. Negative strongholds, characterized by deeply ingrained incorrect beliefs and habits, pose a formidable challenge to break free from. These entrenched beliefs, habitual behaviors, and distorted perceptions persistently exert an influence, providing opportune ground for the devil and his demons to perpetuate affliction in our lives.

Until the deep-seated origins of these negative strongholds are unearthed and exposed to the illuminating power of the Blood of Jesus Christ, you may find yourself grappling with them, seemingly unable to break free. Inheriting negative behaviors such as alcoholism, uncontrolled anger, unhealthy sexual behaviors, irrational fears, dishonesty, and fraudulent tendencies from our parents or ancestors is a common occurrence. Trying to break free from these habits can be an arduous and challenging journey, regardless of the psychological efforts and willpower exerted. Only through a profound spiritual acknowledgment and deliberate rejection of these destructive tendencies can we hope to shatter their powerful hold over us. Let's make a conscious decision to actively reject and challenge bad behavior within our families by speaking up about it. We must stop pretending that such behavior is acceptable. Have you ever noticed that in certain families, it's common to observe a pattern where the father exhibits overwhelming anger, the son seems to have inherited this trait, and even the grandfather struggled with the same issue? Do you ever wonder why you struggle with persistent, irrational fears or depression, and then realize that these challenges have also impacted your mother and her father? It's a reminder that these issues might have a deeper root within your family, and that understanding and addressing them is crucial for breaking the cycle. The lingering effects we experience are the direct consequence of inherited curses rather than learned behaviors. They can be likened to bondages that must be actively and consciously overcome through prayer.

You may remember the research I mentioned at the beginning of this book. Initially, I didn't understand why I had such a strong urge to explore my family history. I started asking family members about the stories I had heard while growing up. Some were just bits and pieces, and these fragments left me wondering—what was the real story? Did I find all my answers? Despite my arduous quest, I didn't find all the answers I sought. It's noteworthy that within my family, there exists a proclivity for tightly clutching onto secrets, even in situations where revealing these hidden truths could have the power to emancipate numerous people from their burdens. I want to emphasize that my involvement in this quest was not driven by mere curiosity. I felt compelled to pursue it because God had been unveiling certain revelations to me, ones that I found challenging to comprehend. Through my studies of the scriptures in search of answers, I came to the realization that this journey was not solely about my personal struggles; it was connected to my family's history and legacy. Generations to come can be profoundly impacted by the repercussions of harboring secrets, entangling in lies, and engaging in demonic activities. The effects can reverberate through time, casting a shadow of deception and pain upon your offspring. However, although I have not yet answered all the questions about my family history, I found what was needed to realize what hold was on my bloodline.

We gathered most of my information from online sources and graveyards. Yes, it may sound unusual, but graveyards can provide a lot of insight into someone's history. In relation to the poem at the beginning of the Prelude, the stanza states, "A life without Christ is plain to see, in the disheveled graves hidden in bushes and trees. What pain did they bring to deserve separation? While family close by donned flowers of celebration." We discovered the grave of a past relative in the woods. It was battered, without a headstone, and so abandoned that we almost missed it. Meanwhile, his parents and other family members were neatly enclosed in a plot just up the hill. Upon researching, we found out that this relative had a very questionable past and wasn't well-liked due to his choices involving alcohol, drugs, and women, which affected the way he treated people. The way you treat people holds significant meaning to Christ. What kind of legacy are you creating? How will people perceive your memory? It will be reflected in the values you pass on to your children. Personally, I aspire to be remembered for embodying the power and anointing of Jesus Christ, and I believe you can, too. Break the Silence in your family and become a generational curse breaker.

There are many types of curses and a myriad of things that contribute to silent suffering, frustrations, and unanswered questions. However, the message is that deliverance can be found in Jesus Christ. His blood and name are sufficient for providing complete healing, deliverance, and restoration from the issues caused by curses. All we need to do is rid our lives of the sins that bind us. These sins must be renounced—walk in truth. Hopefully, your journey won't lead you to desperately searching graveyards on a hot summer day like we did. It was quite an adventure; my three-year-old grandson was with us, and he lightly touched a headstone that unexpectedly toppled over. The girls had a tough time trying to get it back in place. We shared many laughs during our search. There were numerous unexpected holes and loose headstones. Please be cautious if that's where you have to start looking for answers. As I mentioned before, there are questions that we still haven't gotten answers to; and may never find them. However, we know enough to understand why there would be curses on our bloodline. We managed to trace us all the way to Germany, England, Poland, and other countries.

We found Dutchess, Ladies, Sir, Knights, and other royalty. Purchases of land and early settlement names that are attached to our family tree make it hard to understand how we got to the impoverished state we are in now. The insidious nature of greed becomes apparent when it is detached from its origins, which is God, and leads to hoarding and conflict as if it were obtained independently. Therefore, it is crucial to understand curses and their roots in order to gain the necessary knowledge to break the curse and prevent its recurrence in our bloodline. Don't be someone who refuses to acknowledge the truth of what you discover. When God reveals incorrect behaviors, make changes in your life. Although it's possible that some family members may become upset with you and say things like, 'Do you think you're better than the rest of us?' Don't let that discourage you from putting an end to such behaviors in your life and your family's descendants.

Knowledge is power—but you need Godly knowledge to conquer curses once and for all.

I feel that the book of Nehemiah provides a powerful example of resilience and hope, particularly when facing adversity. Nehemiah's determination to rebuild the wall that had been burned and destroyed serves as an inspiring metaphor for overcoming challenges. Despite the seemingly insurmountable task and the limited resources at hand, Nehemiah's unwavering commitment shines through. Instead of being discouraged by the rubble and burned bricks, he chose to take action. His willingness to pick up the bricks, clean them off, and start the process of rebuilding the wall reflects a profound message of perseverance and faith.

In our own lives, we may encounter situations that appear bleak and hopeless, especially within our families. The analogy of using burnt bricks to rebuild the wall is a powerful reminder that even in the midst of brokenness, there is potential for restoration. It conveys that God can work through the most challenging circumstances, transforming them into something even better than before. This message encourages us not to be disheartened by the current state of affairs but to have faith in the possibility of rebuilding and renewal. Rebuild that wall.

Chapter Twelve

Deliverance in Jesus' Name

In the earlier section, I emphasized that this book's theme extends beyond the issue of curses and their consequences. The primary focus lies in the remedy, which is finding deliverance and freedom through Jesus Christ. If you believe that your current struggles may be linked to curses, here are the steps you can take to seek deliverance.

1. **Choose to dedicate your life to following the teachings and example of Jesus Christ.**

   In my experience as a minister and as the daughter of a minister, I have encountered numerous individuals who have fervently sought deliverance from curses through prayer, but with little apparent effect. Families have gone to great lengths, organizing multiple family deliverance prayers, investing significant resources to invite revered religious leaders to conduct prayers in their ancestral homes, and purchasing various items such as anointing oils, anointed sands, and holy waters. Despite these efforts, they have seen little to no change, prompting them to seek out another prophet or religious figure to intercede on their behalf once again. Despite their months-long faith in the transformative power of the new prophet's prayers, they have yet to witness any tangible changes. As a result, they feel compelled to seek out another man of God in the hope of experiencing a different outcome. This pattern of seeking spiritual intervention continues unabated, perpetuating a cycle of uncertainty and a fervent quest for divine intervention.

My friend, there are no shortcuts to deliverance. It cannot be purchased with money or achieved through financial investments in religious work. Deliverance is solely obtained through the sacrificial act of Jesus Christ. True deliverance is received through genuine repentance for our sins and a wholehearted commitment to living a life in accordance with the teachings of Christ. Remember this: Jesus always keeps his promises to us. But if you truly want to experience lasting freedom and deliverance, it starts with you. You have to take the first step by repenting and wholeheartedly accepting Jesus Christ as your Lord and Savior. You can't borrow someone else's repentance for your own freedom—God doesn't work like that. It's a personal journey. Once you've made that decision, then you can boldly seek your deliverance. Do you desire deliverance and change? Many seek it desperately yet are unwilling to repent of their sins and accept Christ as their Lord and Savior. It's regrettable that they yearn for what only God can offer but are reluctant to receive it according to God's plan.

To break free from curses, your first step is to wholeheartedly accept Jesus Christ as your Lord and Savior. This is not simply about attending church. Many people attend church without truly knowing God. Merely attending church does not equate to being born again. What I am urging you to do is to sincerely repent your sins and actively pursue a life of righteousness and dedication to the Lord. If you need deliverance, it's important to approach God with a humble heart. Acknowledge Jesus Christ as your Lord and Savior, sincerely repent for any wrongdoing, and make a commitment to living a life aligned with God's teachings. This initial step is vital in initiating the process of deliverance and finding peace and fulfillment in your spiritual journey.

2. Embrace this truth: if there is no cause, there's no curse.

Always keep in mind that curses can only take hold if there is a root cause. Therefore, curses have the power to operate because they are linked to specific factors. It's crucial to identify these underlying factors that can potentially serve as channels for curses within one's family. Familiar traits, unresolved conflicts, and negative patterns may all act as conduits for curses within a family dynamic. Here are a few essential points to consider:

- Continuously disregarding God's divine guidance is a path that we must not follow.

- Ancestral covenants can be kind of mysterious. You might not even realize they're there until you start asking some serious questions.

- Disrespecting or disobeying your parents goes against the values of compassion, gratitude, and respect that are essential in obeying God.

- Consistently using negative and foul language to describe oneself could be detrimental to your emotional well-being. It's important to be mindful of the words we use to describe ourselves.

- Beware of witchcraft projections, where sinister individuals utilize satanic powers to inflict harm and suffering.

- Pornography is detrimental and should be avoided.

- Adultery and sexual perversion are unfortunately common practices, but it is crucial that we work towards eliminating them.

- Considering advice from witch doctors, voodoo practitioners, spiritists, fortunetellers, palm readers, and similar sources is not to be taken lightly. It's a serious matter with potentially profound consequences.

- Engaging in fraud deliberately is unacceptable and goes against ethical and biblical standards.

- It's crucial to steer clear of involvement in practices such as the occult, freemasonry, lodges, Eckankar, Rosicrucianism, Hare Krishna, etc. These pursuits can have a detrimental impact and should be avoided.

- Being associated with false religious organizations that do not acknowledge the deity of God and deny that Jesus is the only way to God can be detrimental.

- Financial infidelity is a detrimental practice that undermines trust and jeopardizes the stability of relationships. It is crucial to be transparent and honest in all financial matters to ensure a strong and healthy foundation.

- The presence of items such as occult books, covenanted rings, objects used in witchcraft, and materials related to satanic movies should not be obtained.

- Having hands laid on you by deceitful, fake prophets or preachers who have compromised their faith in Christ, please be aware that some individuals may have renounced their religious beliefs by engaging in the worship of mermaids, spiritism, or other occult activities. It's important to be cautious, as there are people who may use occult practices and supernatural powers to influence and spread their messages. Despite their claims, when these individuals lay hands on you, they may actually be imparting demonic spirits rather than the Spirit of God. It's crucial to understand that their spiritual impartation could make you vulnerable to demonic influence. Therefore, it's imperative to adhere to God's word and teachings. Exercise careful discernment with every spirit and resist the temptation to seek visions and prophecies indiscriminately.

- Be aware of soul ties and unhealthy relationships, such as engaging in unscriptural or unsupported business agreements, as well as partaking in sexual relations with demonically possessed individuals. These connections can have a profound impact on your life and well-being.

Before seeking deliverance from curses, examining the root causes of the evil in your life or family is crucial. Dare to confront and eliminate anything that could be connected to curses– whether it's specific sins, toxic relationships, material possessions, or negative emotions. Take decisive action by confessing and repenting from sins, breaking free from harmful relationships, and recommitting your life to Christ. It's time to seek wisdom and make the necessary changes to break free from these curses. Deliverance comes from taking the time to reflect on and identify the underlying causes of the challenges you are facing and seeking God's guidance and support in addressing them. Take some quiet time for reflection, ask God for insight through prayer, and carefully consider the root sources of the problems you are encountering. This self-reflection and seeking guidance from God are essential steps in overcoming the difficulties you are facing. To lift the curse that plagues us, we must actively identify and address the root cause of the problem.

3. Persist in prayer until you achieve your freedom.

The journey to freedom from curses is not an easy one, as curses are some of the most tenacious spiritual obstacles to overcome. Just as the determined woman in Luke chapter 18, you must relentlessly pursue justice until it is achieved. This process requires unwavering persistence and unwavering faith. Once you've achieved deliverance, you will unmistakably sense it. The problem will come to a halt, or you will be filled with an unwavering certainty that the situation is now firmly under your control. If the problem persists, but you have a strong assurance in your spirit that the situation is now under control, it's time to shift to praising. Watch as the physical signs eventually align with the spiritual victory you've obtained. Prepare for a transformation in your dreams - from nightmares and evil manipulations to dreams filled with victory, blessings, and prosperity. It's crucial to grasp that constantly relying on others to pray for you and reveal visions is not the solution. Today, many Christians find themselves consumed by the pursuit of breaking curses in their lives. They go from one spiritual leader to another, seeking deliverance and family blessings. This ongoing cycle can detract from living a purposeful and fulfilling life. It's important to shift focus and seek a more balanced and sustainable approach to spiritual well-being.

Devote ample time to seeking the Lord and offering targeted prayers until you witness God's power being revealed in the situation. Your persistent prayers can move mountains and bring about transformation. The Bible says in Proverbs 6:5— "Deliver thyself as a roe from the hand of the hunter and as a bird from the hand of the fowler." As you embark on your journey to deliverance, remember that the initial step begins with yourself. While seeking prayer support can be valuable, it's essential to recognize that the true crux of deliverance lies within your own efforts. You can be certain that as you earnestly and wholeheartedly seek the Lord, He will bring about your liberation.

4. Through prayer and fasting miracles happen

In the realm of spirituality, fasting serves as a potent tool for conquering what seems unattainable. The pages of the Bible are adorned with instances of fasting and prayer being employed to confront complex dilemmas and circumstances. Notably, Jesus Himself conveyed in

Matthew 17:21 that specific demonic afflictions
necessitated the combined forces of fasting and prayer for
resolution. This underscores the idea that fasting and
prayer hold the potential to facilitate spiritual liberation
from curses and evil covenants. Before engaging in prayer
to combat curses and evil covenants aimed at you and your
family, it's essential to enhance the power of your prayers
through fasting. Scriptures highly endorse fasting as a
means to break free from spiritual limitations and bondage.
Isaiah 58:6 tells us this: "Is not this the fast that I have
chosen: to loose the bands of wickedness, to undo the
heavy burdens, and to let the oppressed go free, and that ye
break every yoke?" Fasting not only strengthens your
spiritual sensitivity but also allows you to discern God's
leading with clarity and conviction. The words from Acts
13:2-3 vividly illustrate how fasting and prayer paved the
way for the Holy Ghost to direct Barnabas and Saul
towards their divine calling. During your period of fasting
and prayer, it's crucial to be receptive to the guidance of
the Holy Ghost within your heart. Similarly, remain
attentive to your dreams, as they may hold significant
messages from the Lord. Whenever you receive inspiration
from God to address something specific, do not hesitate to

seek His grace and confront the matter with courage and faith.

5. Two-minute prayers are insufficient.

Keep praying until something extraordinary happens. Pray until you break free. Pray with such intensity that an overwhelming sense of freedom fills your heart, giving you unshakeable assurance that it's already accomplished. Always keep in mind that the devil, accompanied by his demons, is actively working to thwart your efforts, cause harm, and bring about destruction in your life and the lives of your family members (John 10:10). Stay vigilant and guard yourself against their destructive intentions. Jesus desires for you to experience a life filled with abundance and fulfillment. His intention is for you to live a life of greater quality and purpose. Refuse to accept anything that goes against this and persist in seeking justice until it is rightfully served. Consider initiating your prayer with a prayer of inquiry, a method that encourages seeking divine guidance and understanding of the situation. Instead of simply asking for divine intervention, this approach involves asking the Holy Ghost to illuminate the necessary actions and responsibilities related to the circumstances. By employing this method, you can gain clarity and direction on how to effectively pray for deliverance.

Don't become entangled in simply asking God to resolve the problem. This is not to diminish God's ability to help, because He indeed can and will. However, if the issue persists, you may find yourself trapped in an unending cycle: seeking immediate deliverance, falling into the same sin due to lack of awareness, needing deliverance again, and so on. Instead, implore God to unveil the underlying causes of the issues, allowing you to eliminate the problem and embark on a peaceful journey forward in your walk with Christ.

Example Prayers

Breaking Curses Through Prayer

I have included a few prayers in this section that will help you start breaking curses off your bloodline. In ministry, people often feel like they are not praying correctly and ask for the best way to pray or communicate with God. First, there is no right or wrong way to talk with God as long as you approach Him with a sincere heart. I encourage you to personalize these examples. You don't have to quote them word for word; they are here as a guide.

- **Prayer of Repentance & Forgiveness**

*Heavenly Father, today I humbly come before you and confess my sins. I acknowledge that I have disobeyed your guidance in the past and continue to do so in the present, choosing my own ways instead. I have let my desires, judgments, and human perceptions guide my actions in my relationship with you and others. I have allowed my flesh to dictate my decisions and way of life. Today, Lord, I ask for your forgiveness for all of these sins. Specifically, I ask for forgiveness for (please insert specific sins here). I am sorry for allowing these sins to rule my life. I confess them to you today and accept your gift of forgiveness. Please grant me the grace to overcome these sins and live for your glory from this day forward, in Jesus' name.

*Father Lord, I bring before you every soul tie, negative covenant, agreement, unholy relationship, and permission that you did not sanction for me but which still exists in my life. I ask you to forgive me for entering into these ties, bonds, and relationships. By your Holy Spirit, Lord, lead me out of these unions and help me to see your light and walk out of them. Lord, I ask for the grace to forgive those who have sinned against me from the past up to this moment. I surrender any bitterness in my heart to you and ask for your healing and restoration. Today, I release all the hurts and pains in my heart to you and plead the Blood of Jesus Christ over my spirit, soul, and body. I declare today that I completely forgive those who have offended me and release them from the captivity of bitterness in my heart. Through the blood and name of Jesus Christ, I reclaim every benefit, opportunity, and blessing that unforgiveness has delayed or denied in my life. In Jesus' name, amen.

*Lord, please touch the hearts of those I have offended so that they may forgive and forget my offenses. Grant us the chance to mend our ways and pursue peace once again. Father, if there are people, I need to forgive for my life to progress, please guide me to them now, in Jesus' name. Holy Spirit, cleanse my heart of all unforgiveness, bitterness, regret, self-pity, low self-esteem, dwelling on the past, and thoughts of vengeance. Today, O Lord, I pray that every seed of unforgiveness be destroyed. By the blood of Jesus Christ, I release myself from every form of captivity resulting from inherited family offenses, bitterness, quarrels, and fights. In the name of Jesus, amen.

*Dear Heavenly Father, In the powerful name of Jesus Christ, I humbly seek forgiveness for the sins committed by my parents and ancestors on both my mother's and father's side. I openly acknowledge and renounce the sins of adultery, idolatry, murder, polygamy, spiritism, human sacrifice, agreements and covenants with demons, and occultism as abominations before you. I ask for forgiveness for the far-reaching consequences of these sins and stand before you as an intercessor for my family, fervently pleading for your boundless mercy. Your word tells us that you will pardon the days of ignorance and calls us to repent, and I come before you in unwavering obedience to your divine command. Lord, I repent on behalf of my family, and I implore your forgiveness in the mighty name of Jesus. I hereby nullify any satanic covenants, agreements, connections, exchanges, vows, or transactions made over our lives, bodies, souls, and surroundings by our ancestors and early parents through the sanctified blood of Jesus Christ. I boldly declare that my family and I are redeemed from the clutches of the devil by the precious blood of Jesus Christ. I assert that all satanic seats, altars, dominions, principalities, controls, rulers of darkness, spiritual soldiers of wickedness, and all demonic workings have no authority over us in the mighty name of Jesus. Today, I proclaim that the devil and his demons are eternally barred from infiltrating our family, lives, and destinies. I hoist a spiritual banner over my family and decree that the blood of Jesus Christ is our shield from this day forward. We stride forth in dominion, power, and God's prophetic purpose for our lives—in the name of Jesus Christ. Thank you, Lord, for graciously answering my prayers and bestowing upon us the incredible gifts of forgiveness and healing. I am eternally grateful for the blessings you have bestowed upon me, my family, and our ancestral lineage. In Jesus' name, Amen.

- **Prayers for Revelation and Understanding**

*Father, I humbly seek your guidance and understanding in your teachings. As I immerse myself in your word, I implore you to grant me the freedom, healing, and breakthrough that I seek. Show me the path to righteousness and guide me in overcoming today's challenges. As your word promises, may the Holy Ghost enlighten and remind me of your wisdom. Grant me the strength to break free from any curses or negative influences. In the powerful name of Jesus, I declare these blessings. Amen.

*Almighty Father, Reveal to me all that I need to address in my life. Unveil the relationships I must leave behind. Illuminate the possessions that are not aligned with your will and need to be discarded. Expose the specific sins, attitudes, and actions that the enemy is exploiting to gain a foothold in my life, and empower me, Lord, to confront them according to your guidance. Furthermore, grant me innovative ideas that will establish your purpose for my life, magnify your name, and spread joy among your people on earth. In the name of Jesus, Amen.

*Father, as stated in Jeremiah 33:3, you encourage us to call on you in prayer, promising to reveal great and mighty things that we do not know. Just as you provided clarity to David in his times of need, I seek the same clarity and guidance from you. I believe that you are unchanging and can lead me to victory and breakthrough. According to your word, a curse causeless shall not come. Help me gain insight, revelation, and spiritual understanding to confront the situation I am praying about from its roots. Open my spiritual eyes, ears, and senses, and direct my steps. I refuse to be in the dark any longer. When I rest, may my dreams carry your voice and guidance. I bind and reject all negative influences and dark energies that attempt to invade my dreams and cloud my ability to comprehend the messages being conveyed to me from you, In Jesus' name, Amen

- **Prayers to Break Self-Inflicted Curses**

*Heavenly Father, You have spoken that the power of life and death is in the tongue, and that our words will ultimately justify or condemn us (Proverbs 18:21, Matthew 12:37). Your words are eternal and unchanging, unlike heaven and earth. I humbly confess that I have used my words in ways that do not honor You. I have spoken words of hurt and negativity towards my life, partner, children, family, and nation. Father, I come before You seeking forgiveness for the misuse of my words from the past to this present moment. May the precious Blood of Jesus Christ sanctify my tongue and purify my heart. Empower me to serve as a vessel and proclaimer of life, health, and peace from this day forward. Heavenly Father, I humbly ask for your healing and restoration today, in the powerful name of Jesus. Please mend the pain and hurt I have inflicted upon myself, my family, my children, and my career through my past strong use of words. Grant me the strength to mend what has been broken and the wisdom to use my words with grace and compassion from this day forward. Amen.

*Mighty Lord, I fervently ask for the breaking of any curse that I have unknowingly brought upon myself through my unintentional use of negative words, anger, fear, and anxiety, in the powerful name of Jesus. As it is written, the days of ignorance, the Lord overlooks (Acts 17:30). Therefore, I boldly command any negative impact in my life and family due to my past negative confessions to cease today. I passionately seek God's favor, peace, and breakthrough to abundantly replace any self-inflicted pain

and negativity in my life today, in Jesus' name. I declare blessings upon myself, my home, my career, my family, my church, and my children. From this moment on, my presence will bring blessings, and my return will bring even more. I shall be blessed in the city and blessed in the country. While others may talk of despair, I will speak of triumph and elevation. O Lord, as stated in Romans 8:28, I firmly believe that everything is working out for my good. I am a powerful blessing to my family, a source of inspiration to my country, and a guiding light for my generation. In the mighty name of Jesus, Amen.

- **Prayers of Curses of Disobedience**

*Almighty Father, King of kings and Lord of Lords, I stand before you today to acknowledge my stubbornness and disobedience to your divine instructions. Your word clearly states that disobedience is as the sin of witchcraft, and I admit that I have been guilty of this sin in numerous ways. I have disregarded your guidance, failed to pay attention to your wisdom, and chosen my own path in my heart, relationships, decisions, finances, and health. Today, I humbly ask for your boundless mercy and forgiveness, in the powerful and redemptive name of Jesus. Today, I wholeheartedly dedicate myself to faithfully following the gentle whispers of God's voice in my heart. My soul yearns for unwavering clarity, longing to decipher with absolute certainty whether a particular thought, idea, or plan is divinely orchestrated. I earnestly seek the courage and unwavering faith to discern and dismiss anything that diverges from God's will, while embracing wholeheartedly those inspired by Him. As I take this profound step, I boldly proclaim the promise of Isaiah 1:19, believing with all my being that I shall taste the abundance of the land, blessed in the mighty name of Jesus. Today marks the day I release all seeds of disobedience from my heart and life. From this pivotal moment onward, I declare with unwavering faith that my toil will no longer be in vain. I trust that my diligent efforts and the work of my hands will flourish, bringing forth bountiful fruits. I anticipate divine blessings and favor to grace every aspect of my life and endeavors, in the precious name of Jesus. Amen.

- **Prayer against Ancestral and Inherited Curses**

*Heavenly Father, I humbly bring the burdens of my family's past transgressions before you. I fervently invoke the cleansing power of the blood of Jesus Christ upon my family line, encompassing both my maternal and paternal heritage. I implore complete absolution of all iniquities in the name of Jesus. Through the sanctifying blood of Jesus Christ, I renounce and revoke all curses, covenants, and rites enacted by my ancestors or myself within the realms of the air, earth, beneath the earth, in the waters above, and below the earth. As I am reborn in Christ Jesus, I relinquish all former ties; behold, all things are made new. Henceforth, I beseech the annihilation of any lingering childhood manipulation that seeks to hinder my life, family, marriage, and destiny, in the mighty name of Jesus.

*Precious Lord, I humbly ask that the cleansing blood of Jesus Christ flows through the very foundation of my being, washing away all childhood defilements and breaking any chains of evil inheritance. I set myself free from every problem and difficulty operating in my life as a result of ignorant childhood initiation and evil practices by my parents, grandparents, and guardians. Every demonic seed deposited into my life and my body from my childhood, be roasted by fire in the name of Jesus. According to the word of God, if a man is in Christ, he is a new creature, old things are passed away, and all things become new. I, therefore, announce this day before heaven and earth: I am a child of God, and Jesus Christ is in my life. I have been liberated from the satanic kingdom and transformed into the kingdom of light. I am a new creation, destined to triumph in all that I pursue. I am unstoppable in the face of any challenge. Any curse bound to the covenants of my ancestry aiming to hinder my life and destiny, you are now powerless. By the blood of Jesus Christ, I declare my complete liberation from each one of you. In Jesus' name. I command all familiar spirits perpetrating evil in my life and family, hindering the glory of God from showing forth in our efforts, to be crippled, and to get back into the abyss. Every demonic shrine, altar, and temple existing in my life and family is destroyed in the mighty name of Jesus Christ.

*Before praying, read 2 Corinthians 6: 14-17, Colossians 1:13-14

O Lord, as it is written in Colossians 1:13-14, I declare that I have been rescued from the kingdom of darkness and ushered into the kingdom of the Son, Jesus Christ. Through His blood, I have found redemption and the forgiveness of sins. With unwavering conviction, I make the following proclamation today before heaven and earth. I am a citizen of the kingdom of light, seated with Christ in the heavenly places, far above all principalities and powers. Absolutely nothing can hinder me from manifesting the glory of God.

I declare with unwavering faith that no force can obstruct my journey towards healing and divine health. I fervently summon the fire of God to obliterate every hidden curse, spell, charm, and evil incantation aimed at me and my family. I fervently pray for the annihilation of any clandestine covenant that seeks to undermine my life, family, and destiny in the mighty name of Jesus. (Place your hand on your belly and pray) I sever every evil tie linking me to the ancestral curses of my family and community. Today, I invoke the authority of Matthew 18:18 to banish untimely death, sickness, barrenness, disappointment, and failure from my life and family. I decree the restoration of every closed door, lost opportunity, and precious gift in my life and family, in the mighty name of Jesus.

*Today, I boldly decree that any demonic instrument of accusation in my possession, whether known or unknown, shall be rendered powerless in the mighty name of Jesus. I proclaim that I am entirely liberated and emancipated from any generational curse, covenant, or restriction that seeks to hinder my life. As it is written, "whom the Son sets free is free indeed" (John 8:36). Therefore, I declare with unwavering faith that I am unequivocally released from all ancestral curses and spells in the powerful name of Jesus. Amen.

- **Prayers for Spells, Curses, Occultism, Witchcraft, Wicked and Evil-Minded People**

*Father, in the powerful name of Jesus Christ, I express my deepest gratitude to you for granting me authority over the devil and all evil spirits. I stand firmly on the promise that whatever I bind on earth is bound in heaven, and whatever I loose is loosed. Today and for eternity, I boldly declare my unwavering authority over the devil, his cohorts, and all evil entities. I wholeheartedly confess that according to your divine word, Lord, I possess control over demons and evil spirits. By the strength of your name, they are obedient to my commands and declarations from this moment onward. I now expel all wicked messengers and surveillance spirits from the depths of hell who have been assigned against my life and family. I proclaim utter paralysis upon every demonic messenger, evil observer, ensnarer, spiritual predator, and all agents of darkness scheming to bring me shame and loss. I decree their permanent disablement, effective immediately, in the mighty name of Jesus.

*O Lord, it is written that they shall gather together, but their gathering is not of you. Whoever gathers against me shall scatter and fall (Isaiah 54:17). Therefore, I command this day by the authority of Jesus Christ: let a furious east wind from heaven confuse, scatter, and paralyze every evil gathering against my life and my family. Let the power of righteousness and goodness overcome all evil forces aligned against us. I decree this day, let every satanic altar and court existing against my life and family, raising accusations and counter-accusations against me and my destiny, be destroyed by fire. Every demonic lawyer and judge giving judgments against my life, family, and destiny, in the spirit, wherever you are, I command you all to die by fire in the name of Jesus Christ. By the authority given to me, I nullify every evil judgment and decision made or being carried out against my life and family. I command frustration upon all those orchestrating such judgments against my family and me, in Jesus' name!

*As stated in 1 Peter 5:11, all power belongs to God, now and forever. Therefore, anyone who seeks to exert power and authority over my life, whether physically or spiritually, will be held accountable to God's word. Their challenge is not directed towards me, but towards God Himself. Just as the devil was cast out of heaven for daring to defy God, I command them to be stripped of their influence over my life and thwarted from hindering my destiny, in the powerful name of Jesus. I hereby command every satanic monitoring device to fail and plummet into the abyss. I decree that every witchcraft mirror and crystal ball that attempts to observe or influence my destiny shall shatter and scatter, powerless against the authority of Jesus Christ. You that are watching over me and trying to impede my progress; may you experience blindness and paralysis. Any forces investigating my future, may you fail by fire, in the name of Jesus Christ.

*Plead my cause, O Lord, with those who strive with me; fight against those who fight against me. Take hold of shield and buckler, stand up for my help. Also draw out the spear and stop those who pursue me. Say to my soul, "I am your salvation." Let those be put to shame and brought to dishonor who seek after my life; let those be turned back and brought to confusion who plot my hurt. Let them be like chaff before the wind and let the angel of the Lord chase them. Let their way be dark and slippery, and let the angel of the Lord pursue them. For without cause they have hidden their net for me in a pit, which they have dug without cause for my life. Let destruction come upon him unexpectedly and let his net that he has hidden catch himself; into that very destruction let him fall. In Jesus' name. (Psalm 35:1-8)

*Heavenly Father, I command all spiritual arrows intended or released against me, my family, and my marriage to go back to the sender. Ever grave dug against my family and me, O Lord, I close them in the mighty name of Jesus Christ. May every curse, spell, and charm invoked against my life, and may all the plans of the wicked agents of darkness perish today, in Jesus' name.

*O Lord, I declare that every area of my life affected by curses, witchcraft, monitoring demons, and wicked individuals shall experience a miraculous restoration beyond measure. I decree a total turnaround of all lost opportunities and blessings for myself, my family, and my destiny, in the powerful name of Jesus. I receive divine acceleration for breakthroughs and supernatural speed in every area of my life. I command an overflow of unprecedented breakthroughs to come my way. As I rest, I claim peaceful sleep, filled with dreams and visions from heaven. No longer shall I be oppressed in any way in my dreams. I am destined for excellence in every endeavor, and favor will pursue me relentlessly. I receive creative and innovative ideas that will lead to remarkable breakthroughs, in the mighty name of Jesus. Amen.

- **Anointing and Praying for Yourself**

Take a portion of the oil in your hands and lay your hand upon your head

*O Lord, according to your word, every tree you have not planted shall be rooted out and every chaff burned with fire. I, therefore, ask that the fire of the Holy Ghost will trace every satanic seed and plantation in my life and let them be destroyed. Every seed of laziness, disappointment, spiritual deafness, bareness, sin, confusion, frustration, and setback, be destroyed by fire in the name of Jesus Christ. Lord, it is written that as I serve you, you will take sickness and disease away from my family and me, and none shall be barren. It is also written in 3 John 1:2 that you want us to prosper and be in good health. And in Psalm 107:20, that you sent your word, and your word heals us from every disease. I pray this moment, Lord, take away every sickness and disease from me, in Jesus' name.

It is written in Isaiah 53:4-5 and 1 Peter 2:24 that "Christ took away my sorrows and carried my infirmities and disease in his body at the cross. He was pierced for my sins and inabilities. The punishment and blow he suffered on the cross was for righteousness. By his stripes, I am healed. I anoint myself according to the word of God. O Lord, I pray for your healing power to move all over my body right now, in the name of Jesus. It is written in Job 22:28 that I shall decree a thing and it shall be established, and light will shine on my ways. It is also written in Matthew 18:18 that whatever I bind on earth will be bound in heaven, and what I loose on earth will be loosed in heaven. I decree an end to all forms of spiritual attacks in my life and family today. I bind and cast all evil spirits fighting and oppressing my life, family, business, finances, dreams, and spiritual life into the abyss in Jesus' name. It is written that whoever the Son sets free shall be free indeed. I believe that Jesus has set me, my family, my body, my children, my business, my marriage, and my career free. My destiny is set free to shine from now onwards, in the name of Jesus Christ. Amen.

Cursed Items

Description of items from Chapter Ten

- Witchcraft—The activity of performing magic to help or harm other people.
- Divination—The skill or act of saying or discovering what will happen in the future.
- Soothsayer—A person who is believed to have the ability to know and tell what will happen in the future.
- Sorcery—A type of magic in which spirits, especially evil ones, are used to make things happen.
- Black magic—A type of magic that is believed to use evil spirits to do harmful things (=people who cannot be seen).
- Voodoo—A religion influenced by traditional African religions that involves magic and attempts to communicate with spirits and dead people, common in parts of the Caribbean, especially Haiti, and parts of the southern United States.
- White magic—Magic that is used to do only good things. (also called abracadabra, bewitch, magic

word, evil eye idiom, mystic, magical, objection believed to bring fortune, protection, or good luck).

- Necromancy—The act of communication with the dead to discover what will happen in the future, or black magic (=magic used for evil purposes).

- Pharmakeia---Employment of drugs, for any purpose; sorcery, magic, enchantment, Rev. 18:23; Gal. 5:20

- Omen—Something considered to be a sign of how a future event will take place: Many people believe that a broken mirror is an omen of bad luck.

- Medium—A person who says they can receive messages from people who are dead.

- Fortune-telling—A person who tells you what they think will happen to you in the future—Also called Clairvoyant, diviner, doomsayer, forecaster, futurist, handicapper, harbinger, palmist, psychic, seer, sibyl, soothsayer, and visionary.

- The ways fortune-telling is done—Horoscopes, palm reading, astrology, crystal balls, tea leaves, tarot cards.

Explanation of list on page 106

- Dream catchers are often placed above beds as a symbol to capture bad dreams and invite good ones. According to the Bible, Satan can appear as an angel of light. Witchcraft often presents itself as a false hope and false help. Despite their peaceful appearance, dream catchers invite witchcraft and allow demonic spirits into your home.

- Sage burning – this is not about cooking. It's about the ceremonial burning of sage. Many believe that burning sage holds medicinal benefits, acts as an antimicrobial agent, and helps eliminate bacteria in your living space. However, there are several other products available for bacteria elimination. It's crucial to recognize that there are forces trying to normalize things that should remain abnormal. If you've explored witchcraft or seen it portrayed on screen, you know that sage is commonly used in summoning, conjuring, and creating environments conducive to witchcraft practices.

- Ouija Boards—both physical and digital versions— you are not summoning and communicating with the deceased; you are summoning demons. Remove this from your home immediately—it is not a game! If your children use electronic devices such as

161

iPads, phones, tablets, or computers, it's important to be vigilant for any electronic applications marketed as games that simulate Ouija board experiences.

- Tarot cards are gaining popularity as a way to seek guidance about the future. However, relying on demonic sources for wisdom is a sin.

- Crystals—Please keep the following in mind: God created crystals, gems, and stones, but it's essential to discern the spiritual implications behind these items. When buying crystals, ensure that they do not come with packaging containing statements or phrases with ungodly intentions. Such items are cursed due to the negative energy associated with them. It's important to understand that crystals do not possess the power to heal—only Jesus can.

- Religious Statues—often, people purchase religious statues because they represent luck or blessings. These are cursed items. There is no such thing as truth in Buddha or Hinduism. If you are a true Christian, you believe that those gods do not coexist with the one true God. It's, also important to remember that owning statues or crosses of Jesus for protection and blessings isn't necessary for a relationship with Jesus. The Bible discourages putting one's faith in material objects for peace, prosperity, and health.

- Evil Books—Books of witchcraft and world religions, rituals, incantations, and spells from different cultures; books with sexual fantasy or wizard books; and even fiction books with any form of witchcraft in their storyline—including children's books—are considered evil.

- Evil Toys—Any toy from movies or comic books that depict murder, mischief, and evil—The rule of thumb here would be: when in doubt, throw it out.

- Evil Jewelry—All-seeing eye and masonic rings— they are not warding off evil; they are attracting it. Here again, we have Christian-based jewelry, such as beads that are part of a ritual, jewelry connected to the Saints; Saints become idols; they are dead people—stop praying to Saints! The sacrifice of Jesus Christ means that there's no veil between you and God; you can come boldly before the throne of grace. Rosaries or prayer beads are not needed; crosses worn around your neck with the intent to protect you, is a sin! That chain isn't going to protect anyone! It is having the blood of Jesus

Christ applied to your life. Make sure your salvation is secured in Him, filled with the Holy Ghost—that's all you need.

- Soul tie Objects—Soul tie objects are reminders of past experiences, such as sexual encounters or past relationships. These items like: jewelry, pictures, movies, or concert tickets, hold sentimental value and may stir a desire to reconnect with the past. However, letting go of these objects is crucial as they represent the past and can keep you tied to negative experiences. Release yourself from all negative ties to the past by getting rid of these objects.

Poems Written by the Author

Him

At the sound of His words, the world came into view.
From dust, He created man; breathe into him life anew.

He opened the heavens and flooded the earth.
Shut the mouth of lions, and blessed Sara with old age birth.

He showed favor to Ruth and brought down a giant.
Brought the boys through fire, when to the king they were defiant.

In so many things, he showed His might.
Raised dead, gave wisdom, helped armies to fight.

But then, one day, through pain and strife,
He came to earth to give his life.

In humility and shame, he hung on a tree.
For love and love alone—He died there for me.

It was love that brought Him out of that grave.
All for me to conquer sin and from hell, my life to save.

And someday, He'll come back and take us home.
For where He is, that's where I belong.

I Searched

I searched for peace in the bottle, but alcohol let me down.
So, I searched for it in drugs, but my smile quickly turned to a frown.

I then searched in the arms of many lovers. Kisses were sweet, and words were so kind.
But each left me feeling worse than the other, still no peace could I find.

Then, one day, I met a man who was different from the rest.
 He hung onto my every word as each of my sins I confessed.

He took me in His arms; oh, the peace that flooded my soul.
As I let go of all my past and let Jesus take control.

You, too, can know this peace if you will only let Him in.
In His arms of love and mercy, is where new life for you begins.

Love Conquers Death

In shadows dance the echoes, faint and torn,
Worn-out spirits whisper of grief reborn.
Their spectral cries pierce the heavy air,
A tapestry woven with sorrow and care.
I kneel before the ruins of their plight,

Each heavy heart is a candle in the night.
They tower, a testament to battles fought,
Yet here they linger, in silence caught.
Their weariness drapes like a shroud of dust,
Bound by the shackles of relentless trust.
Generations wade through waters of pain,
Curses entangled, like a fierce autumn rain.
But in the tapestry, a thread can change,
A vow awakened, to tear and rearrange.
I stand, a guardian over their decay,
With resolve that quakes the very roots of clay.
I cradle their stories, their burdens, their fears,
Like an ancient river transforming the years.
No longer shall the heartache ripple and swell.
In this moment, I vow to break free from hell.
For in this life where legacies twine,
I declare with conviction; the choice will be mine.
These whispers shall find release in the breeze,
And the cycle of lament shall finally cease.
I am the bridge from the past to the light,
Refusing to pass on their echoes of night.
This love shall be fertile, a garden to plant,
Where laughter replaces the grief of the chant.
Let history rest in the arms of the past,
For tomorrow's dawn beckons, unshackled, steadfast.
I gather their pain, entwined with my breath,
To forge a new path where love conquers death.

FORGIVENESS

I held up a mirror and took a long hard look at me,
Not on outward vanity, but deep inside where eyes cannot see.
What I saw before me was a very lost soul.
So strong was her longing for true happiness to know.
I watched as tears streamed from her eyes and wished I could stop her pain.
But all I could do was stand and watch as the teardrops fell like rain.
Her shattered past and broken dreams showed clearly in her eyes
They now revealed a pain so deep she had tried so hard to disguise.
As I stared into her eyes, a story began to unfold.
A story of heartaches and secrets that for years had been left untold.
Not secrets of wayward loves or any wrongs she had done,
Not even secrets of criminal doings or mischievous fun.
But yet this secret imprisoned her and kept her locked inside.
And with every heartbreak that she faced, more and more of her spirit died.
The pain of the heartaches turned to anger with each new passing day,
And it served as a barrier, keeping true happiness away.
As I looked into her tear-filled eyes, I knew what it was I had to do.
The only way to find true happiness is to start all over anew.
And for this to ever happen, then I must set her free.
Because the key is forgiveness, and I must start with forgiving me.

New Heights

In shadows deep, where silence wept,
A heart once bold, now quietly kept.
Each dream a thread, unraveled, lost,
In the web of fate, I paid the cost.
Fingers stained with ashes of defeat,
 Every tender touch turned bitter, incomplete.
Hope's gentle flame, extinguished, dim,
As love lay tangled in the curse so grim.
Family ties, like chains of old,
Whispers of sorrow, tales untold.
Innocent laughter, now echoes of despair,
A lineage haunted, stripped bare.
Yet through the fog, a dawning light,
A flicker of truth breaks through the night.
Cursed no more, I stand to claim
The power hidden in love's pure name.
For in the cracks of broken dreams,
 Resilience blooms, or so it seems.
With every fracture, a chance to mend,
 From death's tight grip, the soul ascends.
So let the past be a voice, not a chain,
Shatter the echoes, embrace the pain.
For in our depths, a spark ignites,
From ashes of sorrow, we rise to new heights.

Rich in Love

In a cottage woven of dreams so small,
Where laughter danced through each shabby wall,
I wore a crown of wildflower grace,
In innocence's warmth, I found my place.
With hands calloused by time, but hearts ever free,
They taught me of riches the eye cannot see.
A banquet of kindness, a feast for the soul,
In the arms of my family, I felt truly whole.
Love wrapped around me, a blanket so warm,
Shielding my spirit from life's fierce storm.
No fears of the future, no shadows of shame,
In the light of our laughter, I never felt pain.
But time has a way of unmasking the truth,
As reality whispers the frost into youth.
Yet if love could protect, I would wear it like armor,
A silk woven tapestry-gentle yet stronger.
Though days grew heavier, our coffers ran dry,
In the garden of love, the heart learns to fly.
Now, as I wander through memories old,
I cherish the warmth of a love untold.
And though poverty lingered like a ghost round my door,
In that humble embrace, I was rich to the core.
For love was the treasure that stood the test of gloom,
A fragile, fierce flower, forever in bloom.

Sunday Morning

In the hushed embrace of a Sunday morn,
I nestled close, in faith reborn,
Beside my mother, warm and wise,
Her whispers like hymns, beneath stained skies.
In the glow of centuries, the wood well-worn,
My father's voice, a beacon shorn,
With passion ignited, he spoke the truth,
In every lesson, lived the proof.
"Walk in kindness, let love be your guide,
In the face of storm, let your heart abide,
Jesus, our compass, steadfast and near,
In grace, we find courage, in hope, we steer."
With each fervent word that swirled in the air,
I learned of a world, both tender and rare,
Through sacred tales and prayers softly spun,
A tapestry woven, our journey's begun.
For in that pew, beneath watchful eyes,
I grew rooted in values, where faith never dies,
Though time may unfurl and lead me astray,
The echoes of wisdom will forever hold sway.

Autumn's Whisper

In autumn's whisper, the cool breeze sighs,
A tender lullaby beneath the amber skies.

Sweaters embrace like old friends returned,
While flames crackle gently, warm hearts discerned.

Hot cocoa swirls in the ceramic embrace,
Each sip a memory, a soft, sweet trace.

Marshmallows dance above the glowing light,
Golden edges kissed by the flickering night.

Nature dons her quilt, stitched in vivid hues,
Leaves pirouette softly, painting paths we choose.

With every breath, nostalgia's gentle call,
In this hallowed season, we feel it all.

Season of Letting Go

Beneath the whispering trees, they dance,
Leaves tumbling down in a vibrant trance.

Crimson like a lover's sigh,
Gold like dreams that never die.

The world, adorned in hues so warm,
As autumn wraps us in its charm.

Cuddles soft like whispered vows,
In the glow of the fireplace, we find our house.

Steam rising from a coffee cup,
The taste of solace let's drink it up.

With every sip, the chill fades away,
In this tender moment, forever we'll stay.

So let the leaves fall, let the colors flow,
In the embrace of love, we bask and glow.

For in this season, with hearts aglow,
We find the beauty in letting go.

In the Whisper of His Word

In the hush of dawn, I seek His grace,
Each verse a mirror, reflecting my face.
Pages worn like footsteps in sand,
A sacred journey, a guiding hand.
The ink spills truth, a gentle embrace,
In stories of hope, I find my place.
From Genesis dreams to Revelation's light,
I unravel the shadows, emerge from the night.
Who am I in this tapestry spun?
A thread of His love, a song yet unsung.
In valleys of fear, where echoes reside,
I stand on His promises, my heart is my guide.
His voice like a river, flows deep in my soul,
Brick by brick, He makes me whole.
I am not alone in the quest to belong,
For in finding Him, I hear my own song.
So, I dive into scripture, with open eyes wide,
Each word a compass, pulling me inside.
Finding myself in the word of God's grace,
In knowing Him fully, I find my true place.

More than a woman, A warrior of God.

In the quiet dawn's embrace, she stands,
More than a woman, with faith in her hands,

A warrior of God, her spirit a flame,
Through battles of life, she rises the same.

With courage like thunder, she faces the storm,
In the valleys of shadows, her heart remains warm.

Her prayers are the armor that shields her each day,
In the dance of the dark, she finds her own way.

Her love, a fierce current, it carries the weak,
In the whispers of sorrow, it's hope that she speaks,

With grace like a river, she flows ever wide,
A beacon of strength, relentless as tide.

In moments of doubt, when the night seems so long,
Her faith is the chorus, a sacred, sweet song.

For she's more than a woman, a light in the fray,
A warrior of God, come what may, come what may.

God Fights for Me

In whispers soft, beneath your gaze,
You deem my heart a fragile maze,
Yet in the shadowed corners of my soul,
Rests a tempest, fierce and whole.
You see a willow, bending low,
But roots run deep where strength can grow.
What you perceive as meek and mild,
Is the quiet rage of nature's child.
For in the silence, when starlight gleams,
I weave my power through unspoken dreams.
Each doubt you cast, each word unkind,
Ignites a flame within my mind.
You think me fragile-oh, how misguided!
In storms of doubt, my spirit's bided,
For in the stillness, in prayers I cry,
I find my wings too wild to die.
So, underestimate, if you must,
In God's embrace, I find my trust.
For deeper than any chasm's arc,
Awakens in me the lion's spark.
Fear not my softness, nor the tears I shed,
For in the fabric of my heart, strength is bred.
Beyond your vision, fierce winds decree,
Because I am a woman, and God fights for me.

Whispers of Strength

Beneath the veil of bruised skin,
A warrior waits for her fight to begin.

Each tear a river, each scar a song,
In the heart of the weak, the forever strong.

In the garden of courage, watch petals unfurl,
A phoenix anew, from the ashes she twirls,

For every dark night must yield to the dawn,
And out of the shadows, resilience is born.

A Voice to Be Heard

You, who wear the mask of silence,
Come forth, break the chains, reclaim your essence,

Your voice holds power, your story a sword,
In unity, let's dismantle the words of the ignored.

Let not fear stifle the truth you must share,
For in this symphony of strength, there's care,

We'll weave hope together, a tapestry bright,
To illuminate darkness, to ignite the fight.

Phoenix Rising

In shadows deep, where silence weeps,
A heart once caged, now boldly leaps.
With battered wings and scars that show,
The strength to rise from pain's cruel blow.
A whisper in the dark, a trembling voice,
In fierce defiance, she makes her choice.
From ashes cold, a fire is born,
In the depths of night, she greets the dawn.
No longer shackled by fear's tight grip,
She hoists her sails on freedom's ship.
Each tear a gem, each bruise a tale,
In the storm of courage, she will prevail.
The chains that bound her, now rust and dust,
In the reckoning of love, she learns to trust.
With every heartbeat, a phoenix sings,
Of courage found in the darkest things.
So rise, dear soul, from the wreckage you've known,
Embrace the power that's all your own.
For in the face of tempest, you'll find your way,
A warrior forged, come what may.
From ashes you soar, on wings of light,
A testament to strength, fierce and bright.
In the tapestry of life, you weave your thread,
A story of triumph, of hope, newly spread.

Awakening of the Lioness

In shadows woven, whispers soft,
You see her there, where doubts aloft,
A fragile frame, they dare to cast,
Yet strength, like thunder, stirs the past.
Her heart, a drum of ancient fight,
Beats in cadence with the night,
A lioness, though veiled in skin,
Holds the power of deep within.
Generational chains, a heavy shroud,
Yet she stands tall, fierce and proud,
With every breath, she breaks the spell,
Turning silence into a rebel yell.
Curses tethered, entwined in fate,
She shatters dreams, recalibrates,
With every word, she sparks the flame,
To rebirth the souls who dare not name.
From whispered fears to roaring grace,
She finds the strength to take her place,
A legacy of courage, bold and free,
In every heartbeat, the Lion of Judah in she.
So fear not the quiet, the meek or mild,
For in their silence, the spirit's child,
Is crafting a symphony, wild and bright,
In the realm of shadows, she claims her light.

Whispers of the Heart

In the quiet corners of a cluttered past,
Four women gather, shadows overcast,
With voices woven in a tapestry bright,
They embrace the truth wrapped in the night.
Secrets buried like stones in the ground,
Heavy with silence, where sorrow is found,
Each tale a thread, frayed yet divine,
A lineage of heartache, a hidden design.
First, she speaks of lost childhood dreams,
Of laughter silenced, and hushed, muted screams,
Fingers tracing the scars that were born,
From whispers of shadows that ripped her apart.
Next, a sister cradles the weight of despair,
Of love once blooming, now withered bare,
A mother's harsh words, like daggers they fell,
Creating a labyrinth, a venomous spell.
The third stands tall, with a spirit ablaze,
Illuminating truths in a delicate haze,
Of secrets untouched, like petals in bloom,
Yet, fragrant with pain, drawing forth the gloom.
Lastly, the matriarch, a voice strong and wise,
Holding the mirror that unveils the lies,
With tears that echo through generations' song,
She sings of forgiveness, where souls learn to belong.
Together they rise, relentless and bold,
Breaking the silence, the stories unfold,
Healing the fractures, redefining the scars,
In unity, they shine like a constellation of stars.
For family secrets, though painful and deep,
Can fracture the heart but also help us leap,
Into rhythms of love, where the past intertwines,
Hand in hand, they rewrite the lines.

Breaking the Chains

In the tender weave of time's embrace,
A mother's heart, a daughter's grace,
A daughter-in-law, with courage sewn,
A cousin's hand, a strength well known.
Four souls unite, fierce and bold,
In the presence of shadows, they dare to unfold,
The stories of struggle, the whispers of pain,
Transforming their lineage, they rise from the rain.
Each thread they unravel, a curse to defy,
Tangled old beliefs that made spirits shy,
With voices like thunder, they roar and ignite,
Sisters in arms, in the tapestry light.
A circle of wisdom, of laughter and tears,
Dancing through storms, confronting their fears,
For what once was silence, now blooms as a song,
In the warmth of their courage, they finally belong.
Healing the fractures of heart and of mind,
They carve out a legacy, gentle yet blind,
To the chains that once bound them-they sever,
A beacon of hope, forever and ever.
So let it be known, through valleys and peaks,
The power of love is what each heart seeks,
With hands intertwined, they rise from the dust,
Four women, unbroken, united in trust.

Unfazed

In shadows cast by whispered fears,
Where silence grows like tangled vines,
A voice emerged through gathering tears,
To challenge whispers, to break the lines.
Let tempests rage, let fury swell,
For truth, like fire, ignites the night,
With every word, a shattered spell,
To turn our dark into the light.
Let them hurl their words like stones,
Unfazed, I stand, my heart aflame-
For every curse that seeks to atone,
I'll rise as one, reclaim my name.
The sins that lurked in shadowed streets,
Will tremble in the dawn's embrace,
As courage stirs from deep retreats,
And justice finds its rightful place.
So let them seethe, let passions fly,
For I am not the quiet storm-
In speaking out, I learn to fly,
To shape the world, to rise,to transform.

We're Both Free

In the shadows of your voice, I sense a storm,
Tangled words, like thunder, in an echoing swarm.
You call me out, but oh, what is this fire?
Is it rage or resolve, or a dance of desire?
Your power once like music, played on my heart,
But now the strings have frayed, frayed words fall apart
No longer do I tremble at your artful decree,
For light has pierced the darkness, and set my spirit free,
Madness is a mirror, reflecting back the sound,
Of truths we choose to bury, of chains that once were bound,
But here's the raw revelation, a truth we can explore-
Losing power is a freedom, and I crave it evermore.
So cast your stone of anger, let it roll like a tide,
For I've found my footing, I no longer need to hide.
In this beautiful unraveling, we both hold a stake,
A dance of liberation, make no mistake.
We rise in our farewell, in the clarity bestowed,
Two souls shedding shadows, along a brighter road.
Not anger, but acceptance; not loss, but release-
In calling out the darkness, we've both found our peace.

You Thought You Had Me

In shadows once cast by unseen chains,
Where whispers of doubt and sorrow remained,
Satan held the reins, a grasp so tight,
Yet a spark of truth ignited the night.
Generations bind with threads of despair,
Tales of the broken, lost in the air,
But the light of divine pierced through the lies,
Unraveling curses, the darkened ties.
With each step I take on this newfound ground,
The echoes of bondage no longer resound.
Victory's anthem rises clear and bold,
In the heart of the brave, the story is told.
Satan, you falter, your power begins to wane,
In the face of the truth, there's no room for pain.
I stand unshackled, released from the past,
In the embrace of the light, I'm free at last.
Generational curses, you hold no sway,
For love's greatest promise lights up the way.
So here I shall dance, in joy and in grace,
In the arms of redemption, I've found my place.

Fading Shadows

In shadows cast by fervent faith,
Where whispers moonlight the path of wraith,
Religion's veil, a sacred guise,
Yet hides the truth in tangled lies.

Righteous heart, a noble quest,
Can oft be swayed, can be confessed,
Manipulation's artful dance,
Turns spirit's light to darkened stance.

Malice draped in pious robes,
As virtue's face, in silence probes,
What's righteous root when truth's obscured?
In tangled webs, no soul secured.

But still, amidst this swirling strife,
A flicker shines-there lies the life;
The courage found in hearts set free,
To seek the light, to dare to see.

So unravel chains of dogma tight,
Let love lead forth from darkest night;
For in the open hearts will mend,
Where righteousness and truth ascend.

<u>Shaking the Walls</u>

In the quiet of the night, when shadows weave,
I'll shake these walls, in holy praise, believe.
With fervent heart and arms outstretched wide,
I'll lift my voice where faith and strength collide.

When the Lion of Judah, fierce and proud,
Unleashes a roar, like thunder from the cloud,
Mountains tremble, and giants start to fall,
In His mighty presence, we stand tall.

Chains of despair will shatter and break,
In the light of His love, every heart will awake.
With every echo of His glorious sound,
Hope rises swiftly, in grace we are found.

So let the heavens resound with joy and might,
For in the roaring lion, there's darkness turned light.
Praise will be the anthem, our spirits embraced,
As we shake these walls together, in faith interlaced.

Rise After the Fall
In shadows deep, where hope once died,
A heart once shackled, now beats with pride.
Through poverty's chains and ridicule's sting,
I rise like the dawn, resolute, I sing.

For every whisper of scorn that I've known,
A seed of resilience, in silence, has grown.
Despair wrapped its fingers around my soul,
Yet faith lit a flame, igniting me whole.

This season unfolds like a promise divine,
Where justice and grace, in harmony, twine.
Jesus, my anchor, my refuge, my guide,
Will vindicate my name, with love amplified.

The weight of the past, too heavy to bear,
Is lifted by grace, released in the air.
Watch as the blossoms of strength intertwine,
In the garden of courage, my spirit will shine.

No longer a whisper drowned by the night,
But a symphony soaring, a testament of light.
With each step I take, in faith I stand tall,
For this is my season, my rise after the fall.

The Turning Tide
You thought my heart a brittle cage,
A fickle flame, a trembling stage,
Yet in the depths of storm and strife,
I found a guide, a brand new life.

Your laughter echoed, cold as stone,
Yet in the darkness, seeds were sown,
The light broke forth, a blinding grace,
Now every shadow fades in place.

Lose you did, for chains unwind,
Held no longer by fear's cruel bind,
In the name of love, I rise anew,
Satan, my soul belongs to the true.

No longer swayed by empty schemes,
I walk with Him, fulfilling dreams,
So here I stand, in glory's hue,
A warriors heart, a spirit renewed.

Get in Touch

I am always profoundly moved by the inspiring testimonies from my readers. Witnessing the incredible work of God in people's lives fills my heart with joy and gratitude. I urge you to connect with me and share the remarkable ways in which God is moving in your life and community. Please use the contact details below to reach out to me. Let's unite in celebrating the magnificence of God.

- https://linktr.ee/karenplessgaines
- Facebook: @authorkpgaines
- Instagram: @authorkpgaines
- YouTube: @karengaines394
- TikTok: @karenplessgaines
- Clapper: @KarenPlessGaines
- WordPress: kpgaines.com
- Website: https://www.karenplessgaines.com/
- Email: karenplessgaines@outlook.com When emailing, put "curse breaker" in the subject.

Also, if you would please give a review on Amazon

https://www.amazon.com/stores/author/B07QK9SYFH/

**Where there's no cause, there's no curse. **

**It's up to us to break generational curses
When they say, "It runs in the family."
You tell them—"This is where it runs out."

**You're breaking generational curses,
That's why things don't come easy for you.
You're the one your bloodline
has been waiting for.

Other Books By This Author

Fiction Books

Raylene's Daughter— Although Kurt seemed a little shady from the beginning, his secrets turn out to be more than Raylene imagined. His abuse and controlling ways become more than she can bear. She decides she has had enough and tells him that she and their daughter Nylah are leaving. On a cold Chicago night, Raylene runs to safety, covered in blood, and wakes up in the hospital to find out that her husband is missing along with their four-year-old daughter. As secrets about Kurt's past emerge, tensions mount. Raylene tries to put the pieces together to find her daughter. Will they find her in time, or will fate bring her home?

Lost In the Fall— Alyssa McKinney's world seems to be falling apart. Her husband left, leaving her broke to raise two kids alone. The school where she works is closing. She seems to be on a downward spiral. She has lost everything: her job, her home, most of their belongings, and her faith in God. Gavin Keaton keeps himself busy, trying not to think about the wife who left him to be with his best friend. He has given up on love, but he clings tight to his faith. But when the two broken worlds collide, will they be able to see past the hurt of the past and move towards a future together, or will they hold on to the fear of being hurt and let love pass them by?

Nonfiction Books

Perfectly Imperfect Woman of God— God created us

all differently, so why do we spend most of our lives trying to be like others? Why can't we accept who God made us to be? This book explores today's environment and how it influences our tendency to compare ourselves to others instead of embracing our identity as women of God. We are all 'Perfectly Imperfect Women of God,' made in His image to serve Christ uniquely. This book will show you what it means to conform to Christ and not to the world.

The Long Road Home— This book revolves around a profound journey, fueled by intense emotions. Suzie's experiences with abuse and infertility left her feeling overwhelmed and lost. Her resulting anger was directed towards God, creating a deep inner void. In an attempt to fill this void, she turned to destructive coping mechanisms such as drugs, alcohol, and unhealthy relationships. However, these only left her feeling more incomplete. Ultimately, she comes to the realization that the only path to healing and wholeness lies in reconnecting with the source she had long abandoned— her faith in God.

Resources

- Online Bible
https://www.biblegateway.com/

Nasa Glen Research Center

https://www1.grc.nasa.gov/beginners-guide-to-aeronautics/newtons-laws-of-motion/#:~:text=Newton's%20Third%20Law%3A%20Action%20%26%20Reaction&text=His%20third%20law%20states%20that,words%2C%20forces%20result%20from%20interactions.

- Early German Settlers of South Carolina
https://www.dutchforkchapter.org/auswanderer_early.html
- Christopher Pless
https://www.familysearch.org/tree/person/memories/LTZ1-7QK
- James Daniel Davis
https://www.familysearch.org/tree/person/memories/KCD9-SXT
- Hannah Davis family
https://www.familysearch.org/tree/person/memories/KCD9-SXT
- James Daniel Davis history
https://www.familysearch.org/tree/person/memories/KCD9-SXT
- Cambridge online dictionary
- Cambridge Free English Dictionary and Thesaurus
- Pharmakeia

https://en.wiktionary.org/wiki/%CF%86%CE%B1%C
F%81%CE%BC%CE%B1%CE%BA%CE%B5%CE
%AF%CE%B1#:~:text=%CF%86%E1%BE%B0%C
F%81%CE%BC%E1%BE%B0%CE%BA%CE%B5
%CE%AF%E1%BE%B1%20%E2%80%A2%20(pha
rmake%C3%AD%C4%81)%20f%20(,sorcery%2C%2
0witchcraft
and https://www.billmounce.com/greek-
dictionary/pharmakeia

- **Ouija Boards Evil**
  https://nerdist.com/article/history-origin-story-behind-
  the-ouija-board-spiritualism-beliefs-of-evil-pop-
  culture-impact-modern-uses/
- **Some games the devil uses**
  https://lovethynerd.com/7-games-the-devil-uses/

www.ingramcontent.com/pod-product-compliance
Lightning Source LLC
LaVergne TN
LVHW020353090426
835511LV00041B/3036